THE BOOK OF BOOKS

THE
BOOK OF BOOKS

H. I. Hester

Vice-President and Head of Department of Religion

William Jewell College

Convention Press

NASHVILLE   TENNESSEE

Library of Congress Catalog Card Number: 59-10927
Printed in the United States of America
65. AL 59 R.R.D.

About the Author

HUBERT INMAN HESTER was reared in Whiteville, North Carolina. He is a graduate of Wake Forest College, North Carolina, having received the A.B. degree in 1918 and D.D. in 1950. He is a graduate of Southern Baptist Theological Seminary, Louisville, Kentucky, holding the Th.M. (1921) and Th.D. (1923) degrees from that seminary.

On November 1, 1921, he married Miss Carolyne Louise Geer, of Anderson, South Carolina.

Dr. Hester taught religion in Furman University, 1924–26. Since 1926 he has served as head of the Department of Religion at William Jewell College, Liberty, Missouri. He served as interim president of that institution during 1942–43 and has been vice-president since 1943.

He is president of the Missouri Baptist Historical Society, secretary-treasurer of the Southern Baptist Historical Society, secretary-treasurer of the Southern Association of Baptist Colleges and Schools, and president of the board of trustees of the Midwestern Baptist Theological Seminary, Kansas City, Missouri. He is a member of the Rotary Club and has been listed in *Who's Who in America* since 1943.

Dr. Hester has traveled widely in the United States, England, Europe, and Palestine and has done much speaking in various religious gatherings in the United States of America. He is author of the following books: *The Christian College, At Home with the Hebrews, The Heart of Hebrew History,* and *The Heart of the New Testament.*

Church Study Course for Teaching and Training

THE CHURCH STUDY COURSE for Teaching and Training began October 1, 1959. It is a merger of three courses previously promoted by the Baptist Sunday School Board—the Sunday School Training Course, the Graded Training Union Study Course, and the Church Music Training Course.

The course is fully graded. The system of awards provides a series of five diplomas of twenty books each for Adults or Young People, one diploma of ten books for Young People, two diplomas of five books each for Intermediates, and two diplomas of five books each for Juniors. Book awards earned previously in the Sunday School Training Course, the Graded Training Union Study Course, and the Church Music Training Course may be transferred to the new course.

The course is comprehensive. The books are arranged in nineteen categories. The purpose of the course is to (1) help Christians to grow in knowledge and conviction; (2) help them grow toward maturity in Christian character and competence for service; (3) encourage them to participate worthily as workers in their churches; and (4) develop leaders for all phases of church work.

The Church Study Course for Teaching and Training is promoted by the Baptist Sunday School Board, 127 Ninth Avenue, North, Nashville, Tennessee, through its Sunday School, Training Union, Church Music, and Church Administration departments and by the same departments in the states affiliated with the Southern Baptist Convention. A complete description of the course and the system of awards may be found in the *Church Study Course for Teaching and Training* catalog which may be obtained without charge from any one of these departments.

A record of all awards earned should be maintained in each church. A person should be designated by the church to keep the files. Forms for such records may be ordered from any Baptist Book Store.

Requirements for Credit in Class
or Home Study

IF CREDIT IS DESIRED for the study of this book in a class or by home study the following requirements must be met:

I. IN CLASSWORK

1. The class must meet a minimum of seven and one-half clock hours. The required time does not include assembly periods. Ten class periods of forty-five minutes each are recommended. (If laboratory or clinical work is desired in specialized or technical courses, this requirement may be met by six clock hours of classwork and three clock hours of supervised laboratory or clinical work.)

2. A class member who attends all class sessions and completes the reading of the book within a week following the last class session will not be required to do any written work.

3. A class member who is absent from one or more sessions must answer the questions on all chapters he misses. In such a case, he must turn in his paper within a week and must certify that the book has been read.

4. The teacher should request an award for himself. A person who teaches a book in sections B, C, or D of any category or conducts an approved unit of instruction for Nursery, Beginner, or Primary children will be granted an award in category 11, Special Studies, which will count as an elective on his own diploma. He should specify in his request the name of the book taught, or the unit conducted for Nursery, Beginners, or Primaries.

5. The teacher should complete the Request for Book Award—Class Study (Form 150) and forward it within two weeks after the completion of the class to the Church Study Course Awards Office, 127 Ninth Avenue, North, Nashville 3, Tennessee.

II. In Home Study

1. A person who does not attend any class session may receive credit by answering all questions for written work as indicated in the book. When a person turns in his paper on home study, he must certify that he has read the book.

2. Students may find profit in studying the text together, but individual papers are required. Carbon copies or duplicates in any form cannot be accepted.

3. Home study work papers may be graded by the pastor or a person designated by him, or they may be sent to the Church Study Course Awards Office for grading. The form Request for Book Award—Home Study (Form 151) must be used in requesting awards. It should be mailed to Church Study Course Awards Office, 127 Ninth Avenue, North, Nashville 3, Tennessee.

III. Credit for This Book

This book is in category 1, section A.

CONTENTS

Some Projected Visual Materials

For Use in Teaching This Book

The following list of audio-visual materials will be helpful in teaching this book. In some instances more material is listed than it would be practical to use. In such cases, select the frames of the filmstrips and portions of motion pictures that contribute more directly to the chapters of the book and that more nearly meets the needs of the group you are teaching.

CHAPTER 2

Filmstrip: *Joseph*, Part III
Motion Picture: *Abraham's Faith*

CHAPTER 3

Filmstrip: *Moses*, Part I and II

CHAPTER 4

Filmstrip: *Samuel*
Motion Pictures: *Samuel, a Dedicated Man; David, a Young Hero*

CHAPTER 8

Filmstrips: *The Life of Christ Series; Map Study of the Life of Christ*

CHAPTER 9

Filmstrip: *Power to Serve*
Motion Picture: *Endued with Power*

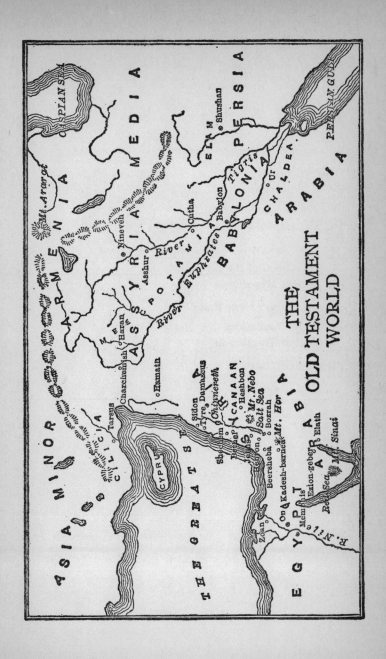

THE OLD TESTAMENT WORLD

CHAPTER 1

1

The Incomparable Book

THE ONE BOOK familiar to more people than is any other ever printed is the Bible. Most of us have seen it in our homes and in our churches from early childhood. This book is available almost anywhere among civilized people today. It is in the cottages of the poor and the humble. It can be seen in the homes of the rich and the famous. Every public library is supplied with various editions and printings. A copy is ready for use in each room in most of the desirable hotels in our country.

The Bible is the one gift most frequently made by friends and loved ones on birthdays and at Christmas. It is the cherished possession of millions of people. Millions of devoted Christians read at least a small portion of this Book every day; millions of others who do not read it daily will admit freely that they should do so. They would agree with the testimony of multitudes of people who have found great strength and comfort in the habit of daily Bible reading.

I. THE MAKE-UP OF THE BIBLE

There can be but one reason for the widespread distribution and use of the Bible. It is because of what the Bible is. It is the Word of God. It answers the need of every heart. It is the word of life. It stimulates the mind, feeds the soul, and satisfies the heart as no other book can. It is the universal Book whose treasures are inexhaustible.

1. *A Library of Sacred Literature*

Essentially the Bible is a collection or library of sacred books. These books were written by different men at different times and under different circumstances over a period

1

of some fifteen hundred years. The writings represent a variety of materials and widely different literary styles. In a real sense, however, they are one Book. Like the human body, the varieties compose a beautiful unity. Each part has a place and makes its contribution. A reader, unacquainted with the process by which the Bible came into being, might conclude that the entire volume was written by one person. This sense of unity is so evident throughout the Bible that we must conclude that it is not the work of men alone, but the masterpiece of a divine Author.

2. *Arrangement of the Contents*

The Bible has two main divisions, called the Old Testament and the New Testament. The word "testament" means covenant, or will. Hence the meaning is the old and the new covenant, or more specifically, the covenant of God with his people before Christ and the new covenant made possible through Christ. The Old Testament closes with the period previous to the birth of Christ. The New Testament begins with the events connected with the birth of Christ and closes about the end of the first Christian century.

There are sixty-six books in the Bible. Thirty-nine of these are included in the Old Testament and twenty-seven in the New Testament. Several different classifications of these books are given. The Jews have one for the Old Testament, and others have been used by different scholars.

For the sake of brevity and convenience, we may divide the Old Testament into three divisions. (1) The first is the seventeen historical books: Genesis, Exodus, Leviticus, Numbers, Deuteronomy, Joshua, Judges, Ruth, 1 Samuel, 2 Samuel, 1 Kings, 2 Kings, 1 Chronicles, 2 Chronicles, Ezra, Nehemiah, and Esther. (2) The following books of poetry make up another section: Job, Psalms, Proverbs, Ecclesiastes, Song of Solomon, and Lamentations, (consists of five poems). (3) In the arrangement in our Bibles, the sixteen books of prophecy complete the Old Testament: Isaiah, Jeremiah, Ezekiel, Daniel, Hosea, Joel, Amos, Obadiah, Jonah, Micah, Nahum, Habakkuk, Zephaniah, Haggai, Zechariah, and

Malachi. The first four mentioned are called the "major" prophets and the other twelve, "minor" prophets.

The New Testament books may be classified as follows: (1) The four Gospels—Matthew, Mark, Luke, John—constitute the first group. (2) One book of history, Acts, forms the next group. (3) There are twenty-one epistles or letters. Thirteen of these were written by Paul, probably in the following order: 1 Thessalonians, 2 Thessalonians, Galatians, Romans, 1 Corinthians, 2 Corinthians, Philippians, Colossians, Philemon, Ephesians, 1 Timothy, 2 Timothy, and Titus. Eight of the epistles are general letters: Hebrews, James, Jude, 1 Peter, 2 Peter, 1 John, 2 John, 3 John. (4) The fourth group consists of one apocalyptic book, the Revelation.

II. The Origin of the Book

How has this Book of books come to us? When and how was it written?

1. *How the Bible Was Written*

There is a wide difference of opinion as to the time when the different books of the Bible were produced. Many competent scholars place the earliest books around 1400 B.C. and the completion of the New Testament about A.D. 100.

It is generally held that there were about forty authors. The Old Testament was written in the Hebrew language, except for some small sections written in the Aramaic tongue. The writers of the New Testament used Greek, with some allusions to the conversational Aramaic of the day. These men used finely prepared sheepskin, vellum, and the material known as papyrus, which was something like our paper. Their writings were preserved, not in the form of a book as we have them today, but in a scroll or long strip of papyrus rolled at either end. These scrolls were used sparingly, were closely guarded, and were carefully preserved.

2. *"Men Spake from God"*

From the foregoing it is evident that men were employed in the writing of these books of the Bible. Although one could cite quite a number of Scripture passages to support this fact, two will be sufficient for our purpose: "God, having of old time spoken unto the fathers in the prophets . . ." (Heb. 1:1 ASV). "Men spake from God, being moved by the Holy Spirit" (2 Peter 1:21 ASV).

The Bible is the Word of God. This word was communicated to men to be put in such form that all men might have it. Thus God used selected men as the instruments for writing his word. These were men of superior endowments and qualifications; they were "holy" men, and yet men who had the necessary faculty for writing the messages entrusted to them. Each had his own style of writing. For example, the literary styles of John and Paul are widely different. Each wrote in his own way; and yet the composite message is vastly more than man's literary production. It is the message of God written by men who were divinely inspired.

3. *The Inspiration of the Scriptures*

Because of its importance in Christian doctrine, many volumes have been written on the inspiration of the Scriptures. Perhaps no one can give a definition of inspiration which would be universally accepted. In general we agree that the divine power which worked in and through the prophets and writers enabled them to record in a trustworthy way the truth which they received from God.

It is worthy of note that we do not have anywhere in the Bible a statement which may be interpreted as a formal definition of inspiration. On the other hand, the fact of divine inspiration is to be found throughout the Bible. We may quote two selections which are especially significant. "Every scripture inspired of God is also profitable for teaching, for reproof, for correction, for instruction which is in righteousness" (2 Tim. 3:16 ASV). "Knowing this first, that no prophecy of scripture is of private interpretation. For no prophecy ever came by the will of man: but men spake from God, being moved by the Holy Spirit" (2 Peter 1:20-21 ASV).

From the foregoing statements we see that these speakers or writers were under the controlling power of the Holy Spirit and consequently the Spirit was speaking through them the message of God.

In general among modern scholars there are three views of inspiration. One extreme view, held by some liberal scholars, is that these original writers were inspired only in the sense that any writer is inspired when producing his best work. By this view Shakespeare, Browning, Goethe, Tennyson, and others were equally inspired and, consequently, their works have the same value. Another extreme view, held by some ultraconservative scholars, is that these writers were inspired to the degree that every minute detail of their work was automatically directed, even to the extent of proper spelling and punctuation.

There is a third view, held by a vast majority of Bible students, which comes in between these two. The writers were men of ability and holy life and were "inbreathed" or inspired by God to write. The Holy Spirit directed them as they wrote the message of God. They were the instruments used for this important service, and yet they were men who were conscious of what they were doing and whose individuality is revealed in their work. They were aware of divine leadership, and because of this fact their writing has divine sanction and authority. It is the Word of God, and as such it has a value and an authority which can be claimed for no other writing.

III. THE PRESERVATION OF THE SACRED WRITINGS

Each book of the Bible was written for some specific and immediate purpose. However, its value and significance would not be exhausted with this particular occasion. The books would be needed for other situations, so would be preserved. Usually they were highly prized and carefully guarded. When one considers the fact that the writings of some forty men were kept through a period of fifteen hundred years of changing fortunes, it is nothing less than miraculous. Indeed we cannot refuse to believe that the hand of God has been at work in preserving these precious writings.

1. *The Canon of the Scriptures*

From all the books written during the centuries in which the Scriptures were coming into being, certain ones were selected and later were recognized as the Bible. These selected writings which met the test were included in the list known as the canon of the Scriptures. Scholars are almost unanimously agreed that this process of selection was completed by about A.D. 400. Since that time the Bible has consisted of these selected books.

The choice was based on long, careful, and prayerful investigations. We can be sure that each book included in our Bible has proved itself to be a part of the inspired Word of God.

The most remarkable thing in the history of literature is the fact that the sixty-six books of the Bible, written by forty or more men in different situations over a period of fifteen hundred years, constitute one great Book in which there are no actual contradictions or inconsistencies. The apparent contradictions, when rightly interpreted, are amenable to reasonable explanation. Even in the Authorized or King James Version, the seeming contradictions do not violate the real message of the Scriptures. Indeed, the marvel is that the various books of the Bible, arranged in their present form, make up a volume which is marked by such complete unity and through which one great purpose runs. God has not only preserved his Word from destruction, he has in a remarkable way watched over it to insure that his message to mankind did not become garbled at the hands of the translators.

2. *Ancient Manuscripts*

We do not have today the original manuscript of any of the books of either the Old Testament or the New Testament. These original manuscripts have long since perished. In most cases, a student is shocked when he first learns this fact. However, his feeling of disappointment soon disappears when he discovers that it does not affect the authenticity of these books as they now appear in our Bible. Ancient peoples guarded such precious documents with the greatest care. Copies were made from the originals as accurately as humanly possible and were distributed to various parts of the world at that time. No part of these sacred writings was allowed to be without many witnesses. We have abundant evidence that the writings we now have are substantially the same as in the days of the first Christian century.

We do have certain very old manuscripts of the books of both Testaments. While they are not the originals, they are old enough to be very accurate copies. Of course, these are of inestimable value. They are to be found in various libraries of the world and are guarded with the greatest care.

IV. TRANSLATIONS OF THE BIBLE

The ancient manuscripts were written in the original language. From time to time there have been translations into other languages.

1. *Early Translations*

The Old Testament, written in the Hebrew language, naturally was the Bible of the Jews. About 275 B.C., when the Jews, along with other peoples of their world, began to use the Greek language, they felt that their Scriptures ought to be in the spoken language of the day. So the famous Septuagint, the Old Testament in Greek, was produced. This was a monumental achievement and is the first translation of any part of the Bible into another tongue. The New Testament was written at a time when Greek was the universal language. Naturally, the New Testament writers used the Greek language.

As time passed and Christianity became the religion of other races, the need for new translations arose. About A.D. 200 the famous Peshitta, a translation of the Bible into the Syrian language, was made. Perhaps the most famous and influential of all these early versions was one known as the Vulgate, made by Jerome near the end of the fourth Christian century. It was in Latin and, after considerable controversy, gradually became the standard used by European peoples. As the Roman Catholic Church grew in power and came to be the predominant expression of Christianity in Europe (A.D. 400 to 1400), this Latin version was used almost exclusively. One can easily see the vast influence it exerted upon the entire world for a thousand years or more.

2. English Translations

With the rise of the English people, there was a demand for the Bible in their language. The first real attempt at an English translation, made against almost unbelievable opposition, was that by John Wycliffe, a great scholar and opponent of the Roman Catholic Church. This famous work appeared in 1380. It was most influential and was the forerunner of a number of other translations which appeared later.

There were several translations which were called Reformation Versions: Tyndale's, 1525; Coverdale's, 1535; the Great Bible, 1539; and so on. The most famous translation of the Bible ever made was the one produced during the reign of King James of England and called the King James, or Authorized Version. This translation appeared in 1611 and, beyond doubt, has exerted a greater influence on the English speaking race, and on the world, than any other ever made.

As time passed and earlier manuscripts of the New Testament were discovered and as the language used in the King James Version became obsolete, scholars felt the need of a new version. So, after prolonged study and diligent labor, the English Revised Version was produced in 1885. The American Revised Version appeared in 1901. Since then a number of translations in so-called "modern speech" have been produced.

The latest and one of the best translations is the Revised Standard Version, which appeared in 1952. From what has been said about the sources from which we get our translations, it will be clear that the oldest manuscripts would be the most accurate. In recent years several very old manuscripts have been discovered. The committee which prepared the Revised Standard Version sought to base their translation on the most accurate manuscripts available and to retain, insofar as possible, the beauty of the well-loved King James Version.

The Bible has been translated into many other languages. In whole or in part, it has appeared in more than eleven hundred languages and dialects. Today there are but few tribes or groups of people anywhere which do not have at least a part of this unique Book in their own speech.

V. The Bible Today

What a treasure Christian people have in the Bible, and yet how limited and fragmentary is our knowledge of it! Today, as never before, it is possible for every eager student to have a knowledge of the Bible. Within the past fifty years the best scholarship has been devoted to the study of this Book. It occupies a greater place of importance and significance than ever before. However great the influence of the Bible in the past on art, sculpture, literature, music, and philosophy, its impact on life today is in many ways greater than ever. It commands the attention and the respect of thinking people everywhere. It is probably read by more people than any other book ever printed. It is the Book of today, and this Book of faith will continue to be mankind's greatest treasure.

VI. Our Book of Faith

Our purpose in writing this study is to acquaint the reader with the main facts of Bible history and to give him a "panoramic" view of the Scriptures. Once the various events and persons are placed in their relation to each other and to the theme of the Bible, then details can be studied in their proper setting, and the revelation of God for man can be more clearly discerned.

This brief survey of the nature of the Bible and how it

came into being will impress the reader with two or three facts. Certainly no other book compares with our Bible in this respect. The Bible is unique in its origin, its nature, and its purpose. Even the most casual reader will be convinced that the Bible is not the work of man alone. In a real sense it comes from God. It has great value as history; it contains the world's finest statements of law; its poetry is unsurpassed in all literature; its biographical sections are world famous; and the messages of the prophets found in the Bible have no parallel in the books of the world. This Book is our authentic record of the history of God's selected race. It records God's revelation of himself to his people. It reveals God's purpose of redeeming mankind.

There are great advantages in seeing the Bible as a whole. Unfortunately, much of our Bible study is unplanned and unorganized. By studying a little section here and another there we are not able to relate these properly. To get even a hurried glimpse of the entire course of Bible history gives the student a sense of unity and order that is highly desirable. This historical survey of the Bible should prove to be interesting and inspiring to the person who wants to know more about God's revelation of himself to men.

FOR CLASS DISCUSSION AND FURTHER STUDY

1. Why are new translations of the Bible needed from time to time?
2. Name some effective methods of studying the Bible. From your experience, cite some advantages of each method you have used.

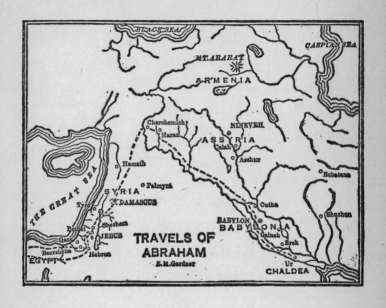

BLACK SEA

CASPIAN SEA

MT. ARARAT

ARMENIA

Charchemish
Haran

NINEVEH

ASSYRIA

Calah

Asshur

Hamath

THE GREAT SEA

Palmyra

SYRIA

DAMASCUS

Ecbatana

Tyre

Shechem

Bethel

JEBUS

Gaza

Beersheba

Hebron

EGYPT

Cutha

Shushan

BABYLON
BABYLONIA

Calneh

Erek

Ur

CHALDEA

TRAVELS OF
ABRAHAM

E. M. Gardner

CHAPTER 2

I. THE CREATION, THE TEMPTATION, AND THE FALL (Gen. 1–3)
   1. The Creation
   2. The Temptation and the Fall

II. FROM THE FALL TO ABRAHAM (Gen. 4–11)

III. INTRODUCING THE PATRIARCHS

IV. ABRAHAM AND ISAAC (Gen. 12–26)
   1. Abraham, Father of the Faithful
   2. Isaac, the Man of Peace
   3. Evaluation of Abraham
   4. The Sons of Isaac

V. THE LIFE OF JACOB (Gen. 25, 27–35)
   1. Early Years
   2. At Haran
   3. Back to the Homeland

VI. THE CAREER OF JOSEPH (Gen. 37–50)
   1. Sold into Slavery
   2. Deliverer of His People

2

The Period of Beginnings

IN THIS CHAPTER we are to deal with the beginnings of Bible history. Our studies will include the record from Adam to Joseph, as found in Genesis 1-50. The time involved is from the creation (the date of which is indefinite) up to about 1600 B.C.

In these studies we are accepting the history which is found in the Old Testament as genuine history. The Old Testament contains narratives, essays, addresses, stories, and poetry. These materials furnish information on the lives of great leaders; on the political, social, economic, and religious life of the Hebrew people; and on surrounding nations as well. Particularly in the book of Genesis, we find much historical material which is found nowhere else. Without these revealing accounts we would know practically nothing of the early history of mankind.

I. THE CREATION, THE TEMPTATION, AND THE FALL
   (Gen. 1-3)

During the past century of our time, the first three chapters of Genesis have been critically examined and studied to a degree probably not true of any other document ever written. Some scholars have sought to discredit these accounts by claiming that they are inconsistent with the views held by modern scientists. Other scholars have approached them with the sincere purpose of discovering the truth and with the desire to gain a better understanding of their content. Millions of people have read and reread these classic accounts with a growing appreciation of their value and importance. These three chapters are particularly important because they are the only orderly, consistent, and valid account we have of the beginnings of our world and of man.

As a literary production, Genesis 1-3 is a classic. The form in which it is presented is important. The first chapter is really a great religious poem declaring God to be the Creator of all things. In six brief, beautiful paragraphs it shows how God, as a creative Spirit, acting through successive periods, prepared the world for the residence of man and put him in it. The record then returns to the story of the creation of man, with whom God is especially concerned, and gives more in detail the facts concerning his creation, condition, duties, and blessings, along with the danger to which he was exposed.

1. *The Creation* (Gen. 1-2)

The Genesis account of the creation is concise and orderly. Six creative "days" are given, specifying what was created each day: (1) Light was created and divided from darkness. (2) The firmament or atmosphere surrounding the earth was made. (3) Water and land were separated and the earth covered with vegetation. (4) The sun, moon, and stars were made to give light upon the earth. (5) Marine life and winged fowl were created. (6) Land animals and man were created.

It is to be noted that in all instances, except in the creation of man, God simply spoke and these other things came into being. But with man it was different. Man was created last and is superior to all other creatures. He was made a living soul, created in God's image. Man's likeness to God is not in his physical being (limbs, eyes, ears, and so forth) for "God is a Spirit" (John 4:24). Man is like God in intellectual, moral, and spiritual qualities.

Made after God's likeness, man is honored above all other creatures. He alone has moral discernment. He was created to keep company with God, to have fellowship with him. He is to "multiply and replenish the earth" and to subdue it. He is to "have dominion" over all other creatures. To man is entrusted the great responsibility of working with God as his intelligent agent in his eternal purposes for man and the world.

To the first man (Adam), Eve was given as a helpmeet, or companion. They were to be husband and wife on a basis of equality. This was the first home and was based on the institution of marriage. Monogamy was unquestionably the ideal, even though in later times men departed from this ideal and practiced polygamy. Husband and wife were to meet the needs of each other. In this institution God has provided the ideal plan for the propagation of the race.

In the story of creation we have the beginning of another important institution, the sabbath day (Gen. 2:2-3). In later times God specifically commanded men to rest on the seventh day. The restrictions were for the benefit of the race. "The sabbath was made for man" (Mark 2:27).

2. The Temptation and the Fall (Gen. 3)

The record of the temptation and the fall of man is one of the most significant and important ever written. To begin with, we must recognize the presence and authority of an evil person known as Satan, who had one vicious motive, namely, to overthrow the work of God and to cause man to doubt the character and the goodness of God. If the tempter could succeed in causing man to question the integrity and love of God, he would have achieved his purpose.

It is to be noted that the appeal of Satan was based on three desires, which ordinarily are perfectly legitimate— the desire for the beautiful, for food, and for knowledge. The sin lay, not in the desires as such, nor even in the effort to satisfy them. It lay in giving any human desire priority over the known will of God and in disobeying God's stated commands.

Up to the time of this experience man was in a state of innocence, but his transgression brought a change in his whole nature, in his relation to God, and in his condition. Man now appears to have become conscious of his guilt, for he sought unsuccessfully to escape God. The old relationship had been broken. Sin had been committed. Now there was guilt; there was shame; there was separation from God and spiritual death.

Naturally, Adam and Eve must be punished for their transgression. The penalties for their sins were stated: The serpent was to crawl on its belly and eat the dust of the earth; Eve was forced to occupy a place of subordination to man and of great suffering; Adam was condemned to a life of toil and death. The condition and the destiny of all mankind were involved in man's tragic sin. "In Adam all die" (1 Cor. 15:22). This doctrine has been taught by the Christian church through all the centuries of its history.

Despite the tragic failure of man in this great crisis, with all its results of pain and punishment, the door of hope was not closed. Man was not forsaken by God, who still loved him despite the sin he had committed. There is a glorious promise of victory to the seed of the woman (Gen. 3:15).

II. FROM THE FALL TO ABRAHAM (Gen. 4–11)

The date for the beginning of the second period of Bible history cannot be determined, since no hint of this is given in Genesis. We can be definite as to the time the period closes, however, since Abraham can be dated at approximately 2000 B.C.

Adam and Eve were expelled from Eden and their two sons, Cain and Abel, were born to them. The writer of Genesis tells at some length the story of Cain's slaying his brother Abel, of Cain's punishment, and of the birth of the third son, Seth, through whom the line was to be continued. Likewise the writer gives a full account of the corruption of man and of the ministry of Noah, which was culminated by the story of the ark and the flood. The accounts of the new start after Noah, the building of the tower of Babel, and the confusion of tongues are given.

III. INTRODUCING THE PATRIARCHS

Prior to the period of the patriarchs, we could not be specific as to dates or geographical locations, but we can be sure of the approximate date of Abraham and we are on sure ground geographically. We can relate these records to secular history, since we are dealing with characters, events, and localities which are recognized by nonbiblical historians.

Competent scholars hold that with Abraham we have the real beginning of the Hebrew people as a race. Abraham was selected for this purpose, and certainly this idea dominates the covenant relationship between Jehovah and him. In both the Old Testament and the New Testament this idea is emphasized. The Hebrew people themselves always looked upon Abraham as founder and father. Thus we are to deal with one of the most significant characters in history as we enter upon the study of this period. With him a new era in history was inaugurated.

It is to be remembered that Abraham, the first of the patriarchs, lived in a remarkable civilization, perhaps deficient in moral and spiritual qualities, but really advanced. There were great libraries filled with volumes, some of which have been translated by scholars of our day. Astronomy, mathematics, and other sciences were taught. Elaborate buildings testified to the knowledge and skill of architects and workmen. The banking and legal professions were well developed, and orderly government was maintained. The solar year had been calculated, and time was divided as we now have it in the sixty-unit system of rotation (sixty seconds to the minute, sixty minutes to the hour). The Code of Hammurabi, 2100 B.C., a system of law attributed to Hammurabi, one of the kings of ancient Babylon, gives a revealing insight into the highly developed civic, business, and social life of these people.

An understanding of the cultural background out of which Abraham came gives fuller meaning to the whole career of this remarkable man and of the significant mission committed to him by God.

In calling Abraham to be the head of a new race, God had a specific purpose. This chosen race was to be his peculiar people. They were elected to be the chief medium in his program of revealing himself to mankind. His blessings upon the race and his dealings with them had religious significance. "In thee shall all families of the earth be blessed" (Gen. 12:3).

IV. ABRAHAM AND ISAAC (Gen. 12–26)

The outstanding character of the patriarchal period is introduced to us by the name of Abram (high father) which was later changed to Abraham (father of a multitude). His wife was first known as Sarai and later as Sarah. The story begins with a man named Terah who lived near Ur with his three sons, Abram, Nahor, and Haran.

1. *Abraham, Father of the Faithful*

Abraham was a shepherd like his father, Terah. Apparently he was wealthy, since he was owner of large flocks and herds and a company of servants. We would assume that his was a family belonging to the higher ranks. The immediate family included Abraham, his wife Sarah, and a nephew Lot (son of Haran). Accompanied by Terah and his family, Abraham, Sarah, and Lot left the vicinity of Ur to move northward to the city of Haran. This, a long journey of some five hundred or more miles, was accomplished with apparent satisfaction. From that time on the city of Haran was regarded as the family home.

According to the word of Stephen in his great defense address, it was before coming to Haran that Abraham received his call from God (Acts 7:2–4). This being true, his stay in Haran was meant to be only temporary. From there he would journey "unto the land that I will show thee" (Gen. 12:1 ASV).

The call which came to Abraham was an event of great significance, the most important religious event since the fall of man, a new starting point in God's method of dealing with men.

God's word to Abraham was both a command and a promise: "Now Jehovah said unto Abram, Get thee out of thy country, and from thy kindred, and from thy father's house, unto the land that I will show thee: and I will make of thee a great nation, and I will bless thee, and make thy name great; and be thou a blessing: and I will bless them that bless thee, and him that curseth thee will I curse: and in thee shall all of the families of the earth be blessed" (Gen. 12:1-3 ASV). In line with God's covenant, Abraham was to be the founder of a new race and the father of a new faith, presaging a close and intimate relation with God. This new people were to receive special revelations from God and to pass them on to others.

It will be helpful to the student to get a brief outline or summary of the journeys of Abraham. From Ur of the Chaldees he moved to Haran. Journeying southward he entered Canaan, making his first stop at Shechem. He then moved a few miles farther south to Bethel. From this point he traversed southern Canaan and entered the land of Egypt, where he and Sarah lived for some time.

After an unhappy experience in Egypt, Abraham and his family moved back to Bethel in central Canaan. It was here that he and Lot separated. Lot took his family and moved down in the Jordan valley near the wicked cities of Sodom and Gomorrah.

Abraham now made his last move when he returned to southern Canaan to establish his home at Hebron. While he later traveled from here to other points, he went only on temporary journeys, leaving his family at Hebron. Here Abraham had many notable experiences, including the visitation of Jehovah under the famous oaks of Mamre. In Hebron, Abraham bought a burial place for himself and his family, the historic cave of Machpelah, where he, Sarah, Isaac, Jacob, and others of his family were buried.

Shortly after Abraham located in Hebron, Jehovah appeared again to Abraham renewing the covenant and promising specifically that he should have a son of his own blood. Abraham and Sarah, though married for many years, were still without an heir. Now, in a vision, Abraham was assured that his seed should be as the sands of the sea and the stars of the heavens in number. He accepted this in faith and "it was imputed to him for righteousness" (Rom. 4:22).

After God had spoken to Abraham, a period of time passed and yet there seemed to be no sign of the fulfilment of the promise of a son. Sarah suggested to her husband that he now take as his wife Hagar, one of her handmaids, since in the promise to him it had not (to that time) been specified that Sarah was to be the mother. Abraham accepted the proposal, and in due time Hagar bore a son whom she called Ishmael (Gen. 16: 4–16).

Other years passed, bringing Abraham to the age of ninety-nine years, when once more God appeared to him and assured him that now the time had come for the fulfilment of the promise. Sarah was to be the mother of his son, but he himself and all male descendants hereafter should submit to the rite of circumcision. His name was changed from Abram (exalted father) to Abraham (father of a multitude). At first Sarah doubted, and even laughed at what appeared so utterly impossible (Gen. 18: 11–15).

2. Isaac, the Man of Peace

At last God's promise was fulfilled. Sarah conceived and bore to Abraham a son who was named Isaac. In due time the boy was weaned. The event was celebrated by a feast, and when Ishmael mocked Isaac, Sarah demanded the unconditional expulsion of Hagar and her boy (Gen. 21: 8–14).

In the meantime Isaac grew into boyhood and was naturally the idol of his parents. The greatest trial and test of Abraham's faith was now to come. He was commanded by Jehovah to take this boy, his only son upon whom so much depended, and to offer him in sacrifice. Apparently God was making clear to Abraham and to all his descendants that the true God was not to be worshiped by human sacrifices patterned after the practices of the heathen peoples of the day.

The test which God gave to Abraham is hard to understand. It was designed not only to confirm Abraham's love for God as greater than his love for his son; it was also a test of Abraham's willingness to believe God's promise. Apparently the command was in direct conflict with the promise that Isaac would be the one through whom God's covenant with Abraham would be carried out. The writer of Hebrews tells us that Abraham obeyed, believing that God was able to raise Isaac from the dead (Heb. 11:17–19). Though he was not able to understand this awful command, nevertheless Abraham met the test. The great man of God proved his faith, his beloved son was spared, and immediately thereafter God renewed his covenant promises to Abraham.

The story of the betrothal and marriage of Isaac and Rebekah is told in detail in a long chapter (Gen. 24). According to Oriental custom, the parents took the initiative and made the arrangements for the marriage of their sons and daughters. Abraham insisted that the wife of Isaac should come, not from the wicked Canaanites, but from his own people back at Paddan-aram. A devoted servant of Abraham, was entrusted with the responsibility of discovering the bride for Isaac. He found Rebekah, the daughter of Bethuel, a nephew of Abraham. She agreed to go back to Canaan with him to become the wife of Isaac (Gen. 24:67). To Isaac and Rebekah were born twin sons, Esau and Jacob.

At the ripe old age of one hundred seventy-five years, Abraham, the grand old man of faith, came to the end of his days. His body was placed beside that of Sarah in the family burial place, the cave of Machpelah, by his sons Isaac and Ishmael.

3. Evaluation of Abraham

In evaluating this man one is tempted to use superlatives. However, the simple fact is that here was one of the really great men of history. Some marvel that such a man could have lived when he did in history. He was great in character and in achievements. His character was not perfect, but his commitment to God made him a man whom God could use. Essentially he was a man of peace. He was generous and unselfish in spirit. His courage is revealed in many trying experiences. He was loyal to the truth and to his family. He was a good business man whose prosperity was known abroad. His good judgment and his wise counsel frequently served his family and friends. He was a man of integrity.

Most striking of all his noble traits was his religious faith. He was "fervent in spirit; serving the Lord." His superb faith in God met every test. The service and worship of God were always first in his life. We cannot imagine a man more fitted to fulfil the duties and to sustain the honors that devolved on the father of a nation.

The achievements of Abraham are most remarkable. Through experiences of war and peace, adversity and prosperity, he led his family and founded a nation. He achieved in material things, but in religious character he is pre-eminent. Three great faiths of mankind—the Jews, Christians, and Mohammedans—embracing more than half the human race, look upon him as the human founder of their respective religions. Indeed, through him all the nations of the earth have been blessed.

4. *The Sons of Isaac*

Esau and Jacob, the twin children borne by Rebekah to Isaac, early revealed disappointing traits of character. Esau (unguarded, profane) seems never to have had a serious mind and never manifested any appreciation for the family heritage and destiny so cherished by Abraham. He lived on the plane of the sensual—that is, of the physical and social nature, apart from the spiritual. He exhibited no great wickedness. He could be classed as harmless, but without purpose or ambition. He did not have in him the makings of a man.

Jacob (supplanter) was notoriously tricky and unscrupulous, with great ambition for himself—ambition which seems to have included some desire for participation in God's covenant. Jacob tried to obtain God's blessing by man's schemes. He could, without hesitation, stoop to deceive his own brother and even his blind old father.

Many students are disturbed by what, on the surface, appears to be the approval of God upon Jacob with all his deceptions. It may be helpful to remember that even God cannot do much with a man who has no purpose beyond the satisfaction of physical desires (even the most cultured desires), no appreciation of higher values, no ambition for himself above the call of present appetites. But God can take a man like Jacob with worthy ambitions, but who admittedly is inclined to deception in his actions, and change his character so as to use him for a great purpose. In other words, a man with questionable ethics but a worthy objective is potentially worth more than a harmless man who has no ambition.

V. THE LIFE OF JACOB (Gen. 25, 27–35)

Jacob occupies a large place in the history of the Hebrew people. His activities, particularly during the latter half of his life as a prince of God, overshadow all other men of the time. His sons became the heads of the twelve tribes of the nation and thus were kept continuously before the Hebrew people in their history.

1. *Early Years* (Gen. 25, 27–28)

The early years of Jacob's life are remembered mainly for his two acts of treachery: purchasing Esau's birthright and deceiving his blind father to steal Esau's blessing. When Jacob fled from the fury of his brother, he naturally turned northward to seek the home of his mother's kinspeople. His first day's travel brought him to Bethel, a well-known stopping place, where his grandfather Abraham had previously lived. At this point the homesick, lonely man spent a memorable night. Here Jehovah, the God of his father, spoke to him. Jacob made his solemn vow, promising in return for Jehovah's favor his faithful service and one tenth of his possessions (Gen. 28 : 10–22).

2. *At Haran* (Gen. 29–31)

Leaving Bethel, Jacob journeyed northward to Haran (Paddan-aram), the old home of his mother Rebekah and her family. Though he did not know it at the time, he was to spend twenty eventful years in this area. Shortly upon his arrival he met Rachel, the daughter of Laban, who was the brother of Rebekah. Jacob fell in love with her at first sight. This was the beginning of a romance which lasted through the years and was terminated only with the untimely death of his beloved Rachel years later, on his return to his ancestral home at Hebron.

The writer of Genesis gives in some detail the experiences of Jacob with his mother's brother. Laban deceived Jacob in giving him Leah, the older sister, instead of Rachel on his wedding night. He worked seven years more for Rachel. Both Laban and Jacob prospered in their business partnership. In the meantime Jacob's family grew; Leah, Rachel, and some concubines bore him twelve sons and one daughter named Dinah.

The years at Paddan-aram passed swiftly, if not too happily for Jacob. He never intended to live here permanently, so the vision of God with the command to return to Canaan was welcomed. After one unsuccessful attempt he was at last able to escape with his family, his flocks and herds.

As Jacob followed the old route southward in Palestine east of the Jordan, he came to the little river Jabbok which emptied into the Jordan River.

3. *Back to the Homeland* (Gen. 32–35)

On the banks of the Jabbok, while anxiously awaiting his meeting with Esau, Jacob had a very remarkable experience. He spent a whole night in prayer, as an angel struggled with him. Whatever difficulties we may have in explaining the details of this strange experience, certain significant facts are clear. God spoke to Jacob, made a covenant with him, and changed his name from Jacob (supplanter) to Israel (prince of God). From this time Jacob was a changed man.

After his experiences east of the Jordan, Jacob moved westward across the river and settled for a while at the old city of Shechem. Directed by God, he brought his family on to Bethel, where as a fugitive he had previously made his vow to Jehovah. He now renewed the vow, and Jehovah, the God of his fathers, spoke to him words of great promise concerning his place in the program of the Hebrew people. "And God said unto him, I am God Almighty: be fruitful and multiply; a nation and a company of nations shall be of thee, and kings shall come out of thy loins; and the land which I gave Abraham and Isaac, to thee I will give it, and to thy seed after thee will I give the land" (Gen. 35:11–12).

Leaving Bethel, Jacob proceeded southward with his family and possessions. A short distance south of the place where Jerusalem now stands, a great loss came to him. Here his beloved Rachel gave birth to his last child, who was given the name Benjamin. But Jacob's joy was soon mingled with sorrow, for in this experience Rachel died. Jacob laid her to rest in a plot hard by the roadway just north of Bethlehem and set a pillar above her grave to mark the spot.

He arrived at last in his ancestral home to greet his aged father. Before long Isaac died, "old and full of days" (one hundred and eighty years) and was tenderly laid away by his sons Jacob and Esau.

VI. THE CAREER OF JOSEPH (Gen. 37–50)

There is no more admirable or attractive man in all of the Old Testament than Joseph. From the standpoint of literature alone, the story of Joseph ranks as one of the greatest narratives ever written.

Except for Benjamin, Joseph was the only son of Jacob and Rachel. For some reason he seems to have been the favorite son of his father. Joseph had two remarkable dreams, the meaning of which was unmistakable, and he (perhaps thoughtlessly) related these to his elder brethren. The account of the dreams, together with the undisguised favoritism their father had already exhibited toward Joseph, aroused the anger and jealously of his brothers to the point of danger.

1. *Sold into Slavery* (Gen. 37:12–36; 39)

The opportunity for his jealous brothers to get vengeance came when Joseph was sent up to Dothan in central Canaan to visit these brothers who were pasturing their flocks. They planned at first to kill him, but instead decided to sell him as a slave to some Midianite merchants enroute to Egypt.

When Joseph reached Egypt, he was sold as a slave to

Potiphar, an officer of the Pharaoh. Joseph accepted the situation, behaved wisely, and soon was in such high favor with his master that he was placed in the highest position of the household. Then came Joseph's great temptation. Although he did not yield to this temptation, Joseph was convicted on evidence which was wholly circumstantial and was placed in prison. In this experience also the Lord was with Joseph, so that he soon rose to a place of authority over all the other prisoners.

2. *Deliverer of His People* (Gen. 40–50)

Joseph remained in prison for two more years. Then Pharaoh himself had two dreams which none of his wise men could interpret. Joseph was sent for and appeared before the Pharaoh. Upon hearing these dreams, Joseph announced the meaning of them as coming from Jehovah his God. The seven fat kine and seven good ears denoted seven years of abundant crops, which were to be followed by seven years of famine as denoted by the lean kine and poor ears. Joseph advised Pharaoh to appoint a food commissioner to store up supplies in the years of plenty against the years of famine which were to follow.

To his great surprise Joseph was appointed by Pharaoh to assume responsibility for the program which he had just recommended. At thirty years of age this young Hebrew, who had been sold as a slave, occupied the most prominent position in the rich and famous land of Egypt. Joseph stored up grain for the lean years to come. Then came the famine, when all the land suffered and people from surrounding countries came to Joseph for supplies.

The effects of the famine were not confined to Egypt. In Canaan Jacob and his sons, like all others, were in need of food. So the ten older brothers came down to Egypt to buy corn. When they came into the presence of Joseph they did not recognize him, but he recognized them, though he did not reveal himself. He tested them by rough treatment, accusing them of being spies, and agreed to sell them corn only on the condition that their brother Simeon should be kept as a hostage until they should bring the youngest brother, Benjamin, to take his place. Reluctantly they agreed to these terms.

These brothers later were forced to return to Egypt for grain, and Joseph finally revealed himself to them and then invited them and all their families to come down to Egypt to live.

Jacob, overjoyed with the news of Joseph, whose death he had mourned through the years, quickly decided to go to Egypt to see his son. At Beersheba, on the way down, God appeared to him, promised his blessings upon him in the transfer to Egypt, renewed his promise to Jacob as to the destiny of his sons, and assured him that in due time his family should be brought back to their homeland of Canaan.

At the invitation of Joseph and by permission of the Pharaoh, the families of Jacob were settled in the fertile territory in eastern Egypt, known as the land of Goshen. Since they were shepherds, they were to keep the regal herds. Thus they were happily occupied and were treated with courtesy and respect. At the age of one hundred and forty-seven years, Israel, the aged prince of God, came to the end of his days. His sons, in keeping with their promise, took his body after it was embalmed back to Canaan for burial in the cave of Machpelah beside that of his father. At the age of one hundred and ten years Joseph quietly passed away. His body was embalmed and placed in a casket and was kept until the time when his people should go back to the land of their fathers. We close this period with the descendants of Jacob residing in Egypt, having been there approximately seventy-five years when Joseph died.

The reader may have noted that all the events given in this first period of Bible history are found in Genesis (1-50). The value of the book of Genesis is incalculable, since it is the only record we have of these significant events. We can scarcely conceive of theology at all without the record of the creation, the temptation, and the fall of man. Without

Genesis we would know nothing of God's plan of revealing himself through a nation headed by Abraham. His plan to redeem men from sin is given first in these important records.

In Genesis God is represented, not only as the Creator of all things, but as a God who deals with men in loving fellowship. God made his will known to Adam, Noah, Abraham, Isaac, Jacob, and Joseph. They were encouraged to work with God in the greatest of all enterprises. They entered into a covenant with God and had at least some understanding of God's purpose for his people. The relationship of these patriarchs to God is expressed in dignified and yet perfectly natural language that could be easily understood. Abraham was called the "friend of God," indicating God's loving concern for men.

The picture of God given in Genesis is altogether in harmony with the fuller revelation given later in the Bible. God, revealed in the New Testament as our loving heavenly Father, is the God of Abraham, Isaac, and Jacob. We who call God our Father by faith in Jesus Christ may walk in happy fellowship with him as did these men of faith who lived in the early years of history.

FOR CLASS DISCUSSION AND FURTHER STUDY

1. Throughout your study survey of the Book of books, seek to trace the unfolding story of God's plan of redemption to meet the needs of fallen man. Based on this chapter, discuss—
   (1) The attitude in man that made a plan of redemption necessary
   (2) Man's increasing wickedness traced from Adam to Noah
   (3) God's fresh start with Noah; man's increasing wickedness
   (4) God's fresh start through the covenant with Abraham and the plan for a Chosen People who would be witnesses for God
   (5) The covenant passed to Isaac; to Jacob; to Judah
   (6) The Chosen People preserved through Joseph
   (7) The hopes implied by an unburied coffin in Egypt (Gen. 50:26)

2. Read God's covenant with Abraham as it was unfolded to him from time to time (Gen. 12:1–3; 13:14–17; 15:1–18; 17:1–8; 22:15–18). Then read Galatians 3:6–9 and discuss how this covenant relates to Christians today.
3. Using a map of the journeys of Abraham as you read his story in Genesis, mark the places he visited.

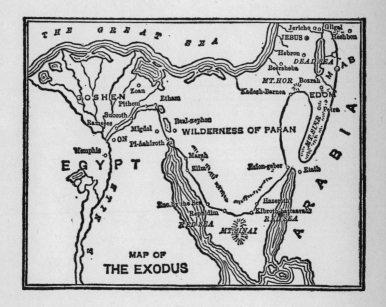

CHAPTER 3

I. IN EGYPTIAN SLAVERY (Ex. 1–2)

II. MOSES, THE DELIVERER (Ex. 2–4)
1. Birth and Preparation
2. The Years in Midian

III. LEAVING EGYPT (Ex. 5–15)
1. The Ten Plagues
2. The Passover and the Escape

IV. THE LAW OF MOSES (Ex. 16–40)
1. Enroute to Mount Sinai
2. Giving the Law
3. Training at Mount Sinai
4. The Tabernacle and the Instructions for the Worship of Jehovah

V. WILDERNESS WANDERINGS (Num. 9–36; Deut.)
1. At Kadesh-barnea
2. The Breakdown of Faith
3. Wandering in the Wilderness
4. On the Borders of Canaan

VI. AN APPRAISAL OF MOSES

VII. COMING INTO CANAAN (Josh. 1–5)
1. Preparation for Crossing the Jordan
2. The Entry into Canaan

VIII. THE CONQUEST OF CANAAN (Josh. 5–24)
1. The Fall of Jericho
2. Conquering the Land

IX. THE DARK AGES OF HEBREW HISTORY (Judg., Ruth)
1. The Work of the Judges
2. The Story of Ruth
3. Evaluation of the Period

3

The Period of National Infancy

THIS PERIOD of Bible history starts with the Hebrew people living in Egypt, about the time of the death of Joseph, and goes up to the career of the great prophet Samuel. The dates involved are hard to determine, since we have no way of knowing the exact time of the Exodus. It seems safe to follow the majority judgment in placing the Exodus around 1400 B.C., though there are some arguments against it. So we are dating this period from 1600 B.C. to 1100 B.C. The chief events in the period are the slavery of the Hebrews in Egypt; the birth, education, and call of Moses; the exodus from Egypt; the wilderness wanderings; the conquest and settlement of Canaan; and the period of the judges. The biblical record of these events is found in Exodus, Leviticus, Numbers, Deuteronomy, Joshua, Judges, and Ruth.

The Hebrews belonged to the Semitic race and were a pastoral people. In Egypt their life was that of a settled agricultural people. The land was extremely rich and the population was dense. Civilization here was far advanced. Slavery was an established institution, and the lot of the slave was very hard. In this world, vastly different from their home in Canaan, the descendants of Jacob lived for many decades. Naturally, they were influenced by the type of life with which they were surrounded.

I. IN EGYPTIAN SLAVERY (Ex. 1-2)

The Hebrew people were located in the fertile region of Goshen in the land of Egypt. Joseph died at one hundred and ten years of age, seventy-five years after his father and his brethren settled in the land.

Whatever may have been the total number of Israelites

31

in Egypt in the days of Jacob, that number soon began to multiply. In Exodus 1:7 we have five expressions to indicate their rapid increase in numbers; in Exodus 12:37 we have the statement that at the time of their departure from Egypt they numbered six hundred thousand men, besides children.

As long as Joseph, their kinsman who occupied such a prominent place in governmental affairs, was alive, the Israelites were in a favored position. But "there arose a new king over Egypt, who knew not Joseph" (Ex. 1:8 ASV). The new Pharaoh, determined to reduce the Hebrew people to slavery, set cruel taskmasters over them and forced them to do the hardest kind of public work, that of making bricks. Under these conditions the sons of Jacob were no longer a free people, welcome guests in another land, but were slaves whose lot was one of oppression and suffering.

Despite the cruel treatment inflicted upon them in this unbearably hard service, the Hebrews continued to multiply. At length, when more severe measures were necessary, the order was officially given that all midwives serving at the birth of Hebrew children should kill the male babies, but spare the females. The midwives refused to carry out these orders, and the Hebrew boys were spared. Finally the Pharaoh issued the desperate command to all his people: "Every son that is born ye shall cast into the river" (Ex. 1:22).

II. Moses, the Deliverer (Ex. 2–4)

In this setting we are introduced to the life and work of the one who is probably the most important man in Old Testament history. Some secular historians rank this man Moses as one of the greatest men in all history. Someone has estimated that one seventh of the Old Testament story is devoted to this remarkable character. He was a statesman, lawgiver, historian, emancipator, poet, and prophet.

1. Birth and Preparation (Ex. 2)

Moses was of the tribe of Levi and had a sister named Miriam and a brother Aaron. He was adopted by the daughter of Pharaoh, who employed his own mother to nurse him.

In this way God prepared Moses in his early years for his future work.

The record in Exodus is silent concerning the boyhood of Moses. In Acts 7:22 Stephen says that he "was learned in all the wisdom of Egypt." The writer of Hebrews 11:25 declares that, had he so desired, Moses might have enjoyed all the pleasure of Egypt. It is not too much to imagine that, as the adopted son of Pharaoh's daughter, Moses would be given the benefits of the best training available to the royal family. We can be certain that his own mother would have acquainted him with God's plans for the Hebrew people as his chosen race. No doubt, as she told Moses about how his life had been spared as a baby, she helped him to feel a deep sense of God's purpose for his life.

The career of Moses naturally falls into three periods of forty years each. The first of these was the time of training and preparation in Egypt. The second period was spent in the land of Midian and was a time of unconscious preparation. The third was the period of actual accomplishment.

2. The Years in Midian (Ex. 3–4)

When he was forty years old, a crisis arose which convinced Moses that he must cast his lot with his own people. His plan failed, and he then fled to Midian in the peninsula of Sinai, a desolate, barren area between two gulfs. Here he found employment guarding the herds of Jethro, the priest of Midian. He later married the daughter of Jethro, who bore him two sons. Here for forty years Moses lived the quiet life of a shepherd. He had time for meditation on the things taught by his mother and for digesting the learning of Egypt. He no doubt learned the ways of the desert tribes and the sources of food and water and became acquainted with the topography of the land through which he was to lead the Hebrew people in the long weary years of their wanderings between Egypt and Canaan.

The years in the wilderness of Midian were brought to an end by a remarkable experience near Mount Horeb. God spoke to Moses from a bush burning with fire, identifying himself as the God of Abraham, Isaac, and Jacob and declaring that he had heard the cries of his people in bondage, that he was going to deliver them, and that Moses was to be the leader in this great undertaking.

III. LEAVING EGYPT (Ex. 5–15)

Moses and Aaron, after establishing their leadership among their own brethren, appeared before the Pharaoh to get his consent for their people to leave Egypt. Pharaoh defiantly refused to grant this and ordered his taskmasters to increase the already severe requirements made of the Hebrew slaves.

1. *The Ten Plagues* (Ex. 7–10)

To overcome the resistance of this monarch, God sent ten plagues to the people of Egypt. The behavior of Pharaoh in these crises is an interesting study. With the coming of each plague he gave his consent for the Hebrews to depart; but when the plague was stayed, he changed his mind until a more severe pestilence was sent.

2. *The Passover and the Escape* (Ex. 11–15)

The ordinance of the Passover, the first feast of the Hebrews, was celebrated before the coming of the last plague, the death of the first-born in Egypt. Each Israelite family killed a lamb, sprinkled its blood upon the doorposts of their home, and then partook of its flesh. The death angel was to "pass over" the homes where this blood was spread. Thus the first-born children of the Israelites were spared, while in all other homes the first-born children were stricken. This tragic event spread consternation over all Egypt, and the Israelites were driven forth from the land.

The story of the march of the Hebrews to the Red Sea and of their miraculous deliverance is familiar. The significance of this event is indicated by the fact that the Bible refers to it over and over as a mighty doing of God, designed to call his people to fidelity.

The shortest route from the land of Goshen to Canaan would have been in the northeasterly direction along the coast of the Mediterranean. The people of Israel did not take this shorter route, since they were to be led to the impressive setting of Mount Sinai, where the law was to be given them and they were to be instructed in the details of this law by which every phase of their living was to be regulated.

IV. THE LAW OF MOSES (Ex. 16–40)

Having escaped from Egypt to enter the wilderness, Moses had not ended his problems; in fact, his real troubles were just beginning. The problem of the organization and direction of this people was a stupendous one. To guide them on the route, to deal with native tribes (sometimes involving war), to secure food and water, and to mediate differences among the Hebrews themselves—these were some of Moses' responsibilities.

These problems would have been difficult enough had Moses been able to count on the united and hearty support of the Israelites themselves. Unfortunately, however, they caused some of his gravest difficulties. Again and again we are told of their complaining at hardships. Several times they openly rebelled against Moses. The patience, tact, good judgment, and unselfish spirit which Moses exhibited in dealing with this complaining and rebellious multitude is one of the most amazing exhibitions of great leadership in all history.

1. *Enroute to Mount Sinai* (Ex. 15:23 to 18:27)

God did not forsake Moses nor his people. To be sure they did meet difficulties frequently, but always they were directed by God and their needs were supplied. God kept his promises and led them in the way.

They were to go far south to Mount Sinai to receive their law before they moved northward toward the Promised Land. After some months they came to Mount Sinai. In these majestic and awe-inspiring mountains there were a number of hills or peaks which may have been the scene of the giving of the law of Moses. Amid these towering peaks, accompanied by the roar of thunder, God spoke to his people.

2. Giving the Law

The giving of the law of Moses, of which the Ten Commandments are the very heart, marks not only the most important event in the history of the Hebrew people, but one of the most important in the whole history of man. It would be impossible to estimate the importance of this law in human history. To the Israelites it was of the utmost significance. For them it was the final, absolute word of God, forever to be observed.

In receiving the law at Sinai, Moses was in the Mount away from the people for forty days. In his absence the people did an almost unbelievable thing in erecting the golden calf.

3. Training at Mount Sinai (Ex. 32–40; Lev.; Num. 1–9)

God directed Moses to go down to the people at this juncture. When he saw the sin of his people, he was filled with indignation. Seizing the calf, he burned it with fire and scattered the ashes in water, which he forced the people to drink. He then called upon the faithful people to slay these offenders. Three thousand were killed because of their sin.

God, in his anger at their sin, threatened to destroy all the people and begin over again with Moses and his children. The intercessory prayer of Moses for his people on this occasion reveals a greatness seldom found in men. God forgave the people, although he disciplined them with a plague. Moses returned to the Mount, where God gave to him the last of the laws of Israel.

The Israelites remained at Sinai something more than a year. During this time they were occupied chiefly in learning the many details of the law which was to be followed by them ever afterwards.

4. *The Tabernacle and the Instructions for the Worship of Jehovah*

In this interval one of the most important developments was the building of the tabernacle, the chief purpose of which was to represent God as dwelling in the midst of his people. The tabernacle with all its furnishings was to be taken with the Israelites in the journey to their homeland. After they reached Canaan, it was to be re-erected and used for the conducting of their worship. It is worthy of note that the general plan of its construction was the pattern for the erection of Solomon's magnificent Temple in Jerusalem. The pattern of the tabernacle is used by the writer of Hebrews to illustrate many spiritual truths (Heb. 9).

V. WILDERNESS WANDERINGS (Num. 9–36; Deut.)

In the vicinity of Mount Sinai the Israelites spent a year. When they were ready to depart, the pillar of cloud and fire moved in front to direct their route. It is not possible to identify all the places involved in this journey, but the general route was northward and terminated at Kadesh-barnea on the southern borders of Canaan (Num. 9–12).

1. *At Kadesh-barnea* (Num. 13)

Twelve men, one from each tribe, were commissioned to go up into the land of Canaan to secure and bring back vital information about the land. They were to ascertain what kind of land it was—its fertility and products, what kind of cities were in the country, and what kind of people inhabited the territory. They proceeded to the extreme northern boundary and returned, probably by a slightly different route. The mission occupied forty days, which was ample time for a survey of this small country. To demonstrate its fertility, the spies brought back large bunches of grapes.

2. *The Breakdown of Faith* (Num. 14)

Upon the return of the spies, the people were assembled to hear their report. All twelve men were agreed that it was a good land which was highly desirable for them. Upon the question of its conquest they were divided. Ten reported that they could not seize this country at that time because of its walled cities and its giant fighting men. Two of the spies, Caleb and Joshua, reported that it could be done (Num. 13:30). In spite of the valiant efforts of these two faithful men, the majority prevailed and the people would not undertake the conquest.

3. *Wandering in the Wilderness* (Num. 15–36)

This failure of the people to exercise faith, when for every reason they should have trusted God, who had so often delivered them in their need, was a grievous sin which must be punished. The ten unfaithful spies were instantly killed by a plague. The people were to wander in the wilderness forty long years. Except for Joshua and Caleb, every one of that generation (above twenty years of age) was to die before the nation finally came into the Promised Land.

It should be said in this connection that the Exodus should have been completed within at least two years; the forty years' wandering was not a part of the original plan, but was punishment for the sin of faithlessness. These unhappy years were years of rebellion and suffering for all. Miriam and Aaron were taken by death. Moses made his great mistake (Num. 20:2–13) which was punished by his not being permitted to lead the Israelites into the land of Canaan. But through it all, God's grace did not fail (Deut. 32:9–12).

4. *On the Borders of Canaan* (Num. 33–36; Deut.)

At long last the children of Israel began their last advance toward the Promised Land, which took them south of Edom and east of the Dead Sea. In this march they defeated the Amorites, the King of Og, the Moabites, and the Midianites, thus gaining possession of much of Palestine east of the Jordan. God now announced to Moses that his work was completed and that he must select Joshua as his successor. When this was done, Moses assembled the people for a long and touching farewell address, after which he was taken up to Mount Pisgah, east of the Dead Sea, where he was given a view of the Land of Promise soon to be occupied by his people. God then took Moses home and placed his body in a tomb, never to be known by men.

VI. An Appraisal of Moses

It is impossible in brief space to make an adequate appraisal of a man so distinguished as Moses. He was the greatest man in Hebrew history. The long record of his achievements is still almost unbelievable. In character he was pre-eminent. He possessed the qualities of personal greatness. Superb courage, patience, unselfishness, forgiveness, meekness (unselfish disinterestedness), integrity, vision, faith, and loyalty are all nobly exhibited in the life of this remarkable man.

His work surpasses that of any other biblical character except Jesus Christ. By any standard Moses would be considered one of the most amazing men in human history.

> The Hebrew lawgiver was a man, who, considered merely in a historical light, without any reference to his Divine inspiration, has exercised a more extensive and permanent influence over the destinies of his own nation and mankind at large, than any other individual recorded in the annals of the world.[1]

He was lawgiver, statesman, judge, warrior, prophet, priest, and poet. To him, more than to any other man, belongs the credit for molding and leading the Hebrew people into a nation. A lesser figure could not have achieved this remarkable goal. Before his departure Moses was able to look upon a mighty people, ready now to enter the Promised Land, where they could begin to fulfil their mission as God's chosen people.

VII. Coming into Canaan (Josh. 1–5)

It will be recalled that Moses, just before his death in Moab, did much in getting the Hebrews ready for the important venture of crossing the Jordan and conquering western Palestine. Joshua, the son of Nun, was selected and was instructed by Moses to be the leader of the Israelites.

1. Preparation for Crossing the Jordan (Josh. 1–2)

Upon the death of Moses, Joshua assumed command and began at once his plans for the big task ahead. As the Israelites, encamped east of the Jordan, made final preparations for the last stages of their venture, there was an air of expectancy among them. At last, after the bitter years of bondage and wilderness wanderings, they were on the threshold of their new home.

Across the Jordan, at the foot of the mountains of western Canaan, lay the strategic city of Jericho, commanding the main pass up into the mountains. It was necessary, therefore, that this strongly fortified city should be taken first. In order to proceed intelligently it was essential that Joshua have accurate and detailed information about this city and the regions round about. Accordingly two spies were selected and sent across the river to reconnoiter this strategic city. After they were befriended by Rahab and had secured the desired information, they proceeded to make their way back across the Jordan to report to Joshua.

In the meantime Joshua was making final plans with his people. Food was provided, the order of the march was arranged, and the people were given instructions for any exigency ahead.

2. The Entry into Canaan (Josh. 3:1 to 5:13)

The time had now come for the decisive move. Early in the morning, which was four days before the time of the Passover, they left their camp and came down to the Jordan. The priests bore the ark of the covenant and marched three thousand feet in front of the people. As they reached the banks and stepped into the waters of the river, which at this season overflowed its banks, "the waters which came down from above stood, and rose up in one heap, a great way off, at Adam, the city that is beside Zarethan; and those that went down toward the sea of the Arabah, even the Salt Sea, were wholly cut off: and the people passed over right against Jericho" (Josh. 3:16 ASV).

The rite of circumcision, commanded of Abraham, but for a long time neglected, was performed. This was followed by the celebration of the Passover on the evening of the fourteenth day of Nisan. After this, the supply of manna which Jehovah had provided ceased. The Exodus was over.

VIII. The Conquest of Canaan (Josh. 5–24)

1. *The Fall of Jericho* (Josh. 5:13 to 6:27)

The important city of Jericho stood some six miles west of the Jordan. This elevated city with its high walls must have appeared well-nigh impregnable to the Hebrews as they advanced westward from the Jordan. It would be fatal to leave such a fortified city in the hands of their enemies. Jericho was indeed a key city.

To Joshua there appeared one who called himself "captain of the host of the Lord" (Josh. 5:14) and who outlined the plan for the conquest of Jericho. Joshua and his people followed the divine instructions, and on the seventh day the proud city was reduced to ruins and the first step in the conquest of western Canaan was successfully taken.

2. *Conquering the Land* (Josh. 7–24)

By reading the records of succeeding encounters, it is easy to discern the general plan of conquest followed by the Hebrews. Their strategy was to move directly west toward the Mediterranean Sea, conquering a strip of territory through the center of the land. This would forestall any possibility of the peoples of the south and the north joining their forces to offer united resistance to the Hebrews. This plan to divide and conquer proved to be effective. Joshua's forces, upon completing their drive to the west, turned southward and eliminated their leading enemies in this direction. Later they advanced northward, subduing their opponents in this area. The last real battle of the conquest was fought far in the north near the waters of the little lake Merom, a few miles north of the Sea of Galilee.

It should be noted that, while the conquest of the land was regarded as complete (Josh. 21:43), the many local tribes were allowed to live by the Hebrews as neighbors. The fact that these Canaanite tribes were not exterminated was crucial to all that followed in Israel (Judg. 3:1).

Under the leadership of Joshua, the law of Moses was ratified at Shechem. The land was then divided among the twelve tribes, and the people began their settled life in the land given to Abraham, their forefather.

When the tribes had settled in their new homes, the career of Joshua, the great soldier and leader, came to an end. Having been warned of the imminence of his departure, he called for an assembly of the chief officials and leaders of the nation at ancient Shechem. In his address on this impressive and historic occasion, Joshua reviewed briefly the big events in their national history and traced the protection and guidance of Jehovah their God in their life as a nation. He then challenged the people to pledge themselves anew to the service of Jehovah. The people solemnly renewed the covenant, whereupon Joshua set up a stone pillar as a memorial of this event.

Shortly after the assembly at Shechem, Joshua, now one hundred ten years of age, came peacefully to the end of his days. He had served his people with great devotion at a critical time in their history. He followed Israel's greatest statesman, Moses, and naturally was somewhat overshadowed by him, but his contribution was significant, and in his own name he stands out as very remarkable.

IX. THE DARK AGES OF HEBREW HISTORY (Judg., Ruth)

The period which we now consider is known as the dark ages of Hebrew history. It is characterized by such words as apostasy, decline, disorder, and demoralization. It was a time of decline in all areas of life—economic, political, social, moral, and religious.

1. *The Work of the Judges* (Judg. 1–21)

The book of Judges relates the stories of a number of leaders called judges. Each story follows the same pattern. It may be called history repeating itself in four stages or steps: (1) the people of God doing evil; (2) Jehovah sending an oppressor to persecute and enslave them; (3) the people in distress praying for deliverance; and (4) God raising up a judge or deliverer to defeat the enemy and free the people.

The chief function of these judges was to serve as military leaders to deliver the people from their oppressors. They served very largely in local crises. They were not leaders of all twelve tribes, and were not, like kings, elected to succeed each other. There probably were times when no judge was serving; at times two or more might be contemporary.

Usually the number is listed as the twelve following: (1) Othniel of Judah; (2) Ehud of Benjamin; (3) Deborah, the prophetess, and Barak; (4) Gideon from Manasseh; (5) Abimelech, son of Gideon; (6) Jair of Gilead; (7) Tola of Issachar; (8) Jephthah of Gilead; (9) Ibzan from Bethlehem; (10) Elan of Zebulon; (11) Abdon; (12) Samson of Dan.

Since it is impossible to give even a summary of the activities of these judges, we must be content simply to list some six of them with the oppressor which each defeated in order to bring freedom to his people.

Othniel of Judah delivered his people from the oppression of the Mesopotamians.

Ehud, the Benjaminite, killed King Eglon and defeated the Moabites.

Deborah and Barak raised an army and in battle defeated the Canaanites who were oppressing the people of Ephraim and northern Canaan.

Gideon from Manasseh led in a successful battle against the Midianites east of the Jordan.

Jephthah, a crude, fierce fighter from east of the Jordan, led an army of men from Judah, Benjamin, and Ephraim, and defeated the Ammonites.

Samson, a Danite, was given supernatural strength to fight against the Philistines, but he never accepted responsibility for leadership and instead wasted his strength in selfish indulgence.

2. *The Story of Ruth* (Ruth 1–4)

The most beautiful, wholesome, and encouraging of all the stories from the time of the judges is that contained in the book of Ruth. It came probably at the close of the period. Ruth could not be classed as a judge, but her story indicates that even in the darkest periods there are always some homes where the choicest values of life are cherished and preserved. It also shows the hand of God at work in a dark period of history, preserving the line through which ultimately the promised Deliverer was to come into the world.

3. *Evaluation of the Period*

We may think of this period as closing somewhere between 1200 and 1100 B.C. The next period marks the beginning of brighter and better days.

This period of biblical history was marked by a remarkable development of Israel as a nation. That which had been promised to Abraham was here taking form. Those Israelites who had escaped from Egypt were largely ignorant of God's purpose for them. The hard years of the Exodus did much to mold them into a nation. But the chief factor in this development was the giving of the law to Moses at Mount Sinai and the period of detailed instruction of the people in this law that followed while at Sinai. Moses, their leader, in various ways contributed to their understanding of this mission. The many acts of God on their behalf during the Exodus gave to the people a better appreciation of their God and of what he expected of them.

We recognize the fact that God had a special mission for the Hebrew people as a nation. At the same time we may be confident that God is concerned about the character and contribution of all nations. Throughout the Bible, God is represented as the God of history. He uses the nations to work out his eternal purposes. The prophets emphatically declared that he used pagan people like the Assyrians to punish his own sinful people, because as God he controls all nations. We may see, therefore, that the same general principles used in dealing with Israel as a nation are applicable today. Obedience to God brings its rewards while disobedience brings punishment and suffering. This fact places heavy responsibility on the leaders of every nation. Today, as always, it may be said, "Blessed is the nation whose God is the Lord" (Psalm 33:12).

FOR CLASS DISCUSSION AND FURTHER STUDY

1. As you continue to trace the unfolding story of God's plan of redemption, note—
   (1) How God worked through slavery and hardship to keep his people from being absorbed into Egyptian culture; to train them for survival in the desert
   (2) How the law served to unify God's people and further prepare them to be his witnesses to the world
   (3) How the knowledge of Jehovah was kept alive by individual witnesses during the days of the conquest and the period of the judges
2. Using a good Bible dictionary, seek to discover information about the religion of the Egyptians that will help you to see how the ten plagues were demonstrations of the power of the true God over the false gods of the land.
3. State all the reasons you can discover to show why Moses is considered such an important character in biblical history and in his influence on the human race.

---

[1] Stanley Lectures on Jewish History, pp. 199-200. Out of print.

CHAPTER 4

I. SAMUEL—PROPHET, PRIEST, STATESMAN (1 Sam. 1–8)
  1. Early Years
  2. The Leader of Israel

II. SAUL, THE FIRST KING (1 Sam. 9–18)
  1. The Demand for a King
  2. Saul, the Military Leader
  3. Saul's Sin and Rejection
  4. The Death of Saul
  5. Evaluation of Saul's Career

III. DAVID, ISRAEL'S GREATEST KING (1 Sam. 19–31; 2 Sam. 1–24; 1 Kings 1–2; 1 Chron. 10–29)
  1. His Early Years
  2. David Becomes King
  3. David's Conquests
  4. David's Great Sin
  5. His Closing Years

IV. SOLOMON, THE KING OF NATIONAL SPLENDOR (1 Kings 1–11; 2 Chron. 1–9)
  1. His Auspicious Start
  2. His Building Enterprises
  3. The Mistakes of Solomon

V. SUMMARY OF THE PERIOD

4

The Period of National Maturity

THE PERIOD which we are now to consider covered something more than one hundred years. It began with the closing years of the judges and terminated with the death of Solomon around 950 B.C. Its significance, however, is out of all proportion to its length. During this period the life of the Hebrew nation underwent a very radical change. In the beginning they were a group of scattered and unorganized tribes, having no vital connection with each other, living almost as separate peoples. At the death of Solomon, the Hebrew nation had attained its highest rank as a nation of wealth and fame. All areas of life, economic, political, social, and religious, were genuinely affected during this time.

I. SAMUEL—PROPHET, PRIEST, STATESMAN (1 Sam. 1-8)

The transition from the dark and chaotic days of the judges to the glorious era of the kings was effected largely through the life and influence of one man, Samuel. He spanned the chasm between the two, closing one period and opening another. The biblical account of these eventful years is found in 1 and 2 Samuel, 1 and 2 Kings, and 1 and 2 Chronicles.

1. Early Years (1 Sam. 1 to 3:18)

The story of the birth, boyhood, and training of this leader is both familiar and inspiring. It centers around his noble mother, Hannah, and Eli the aged priest. The boy was born in answer to prayer, was lovingly nurtured by his devout mother, and at an early age was turned over to Eli in fulfilment of Hannah's vow. Here Samuel grew up as an attendant of the priest. Here in the quiet of night he received his call to become a special servant of God. As Eli grew more feeble and his sons continued in their wicked course, people began to turn to the promising young man, Samuel. About twenty years passed, and we see him acting as leader of the Israelites in their great assembly at Mizpeh. He was the leader of a religious reformation and was accepted as a prophet of deep spiritual life. He was now ready to lead the nation in the crisis caused by the advance of the Philistines.

In the disastrous encounter with the Philistines, the Hebrews were defeated. Eli and his two sons were taken by death. In the next attack, some years later, the Philistines were defeated, and Samuel became leader in all Israel.

2. *The Leader of Israel* (1 Sam. 3:19 to 8:22)

As judge, Samuel was chief advisor in all political and judicial questions. He proved himself an able statesman, well informed on all issues, fair and impartial in his decisions. He enjoyed the unquestioned confidence of all the people, which placed him in a position to exercise far-reaching influence on the destinies of his nation. As priest and prophet he was the responsible leader in the religious life of his people. His home was at Ramah but he established "offices" at three other nearby centers: Bethel, Gilgal, and Mizpah. Upon his official visits to these places he served in two capacities, political and religious.

A man of genuine piety and sincere devotion to Jehovah, Samuel gave active leadership to the religious life of the people. At his official posts, Ramah, Shiloh, Gilgal, and Mizpah, he established schools of the prophets. In this way promising young men were brought together to live and study under the direction of a prophet or teacher. Undoubtedly these schools were largely responsible for the improved conditions that were to come in the political, moral, and religious life of the people of Israel.

II. SAUL, THE FIRST KING (1 Sam. 9–18)

Because the career of Samuel extends far over into the reign of Saul, we shall complete his story as we treat the work of the first king.

1. *The Demand for a King* (1 Sam. 8:1 to 11:15)

As Samuel advanced in years there grew a strong demand among the people for a king. They wanted to be like other nations. They felt that such a form of government would give them strength in dealing with other peoples. They were already attracted by the pomp and splendor of an Oriental court. At first Samuel resisted the demand, but later he yielded to it. He warned the people against the dangers and then agreed to help set up such a government. A series of events (1 Sam. 9:15 to 11:15) led to the general agreement that Saul, a young man of the tribe of Benjamin, should be given this honor and responsibility.

In certain respects Saul was qualified for his new honor. He was a man of large physique and attractive appearance, "higher than any of the people from his shoulders and upward" (1 Sam. 10:23). When he first appeared, he was modest and humble; he did not seek the office and apparently was not eager to serve. In the beginning his humility and obedience to God were very commendable. Undoubtedly he had qualities of real leadership; he had the ability to organize and to execute; he was an able military leader, as is indicated by his decisive victories early in his career.

The situation offered him a great opportunity. He was the first king, the one to blaze the trail, to set the pattern for later rulers. He was all but unanimously accepted. He had the benefits of the wise counsel and the valuable experience of Samuel, the honored and respected leader for so many years.

2. *Saul, the Military Leader* (1 Sam. 11; 13–15; 17–25)

Shortly after Saul's public election, a situation developed which offered him an ideal opportunity to prove his worth and to establish himself with his people by defeating the Ammonites at the city of Jabesh-gilead. This decisive victory caused all Israel to turn to their new king with undivided loyalty. He had proved himself.

According to the biblical record, Saul led in seven military campaigns: (1) against the Ammonites at Jabesh-gilead (1 Sam. 11); (2) against the Philistines (1 Sam. 13–14); (3) several against Moab, Edom, and Zobah (1 Sam. 14:47–52); (4) against the Amalekites (1 Sam. 15); (5) against the Philistines under Goliath (1 Sam. 17); (6) against David in long and unjustified pursuits (1 Sam. 18–23); (7) against the Philistines at Mount Gilboa, which resulted in his death (1 Sam. 24–25).

3. Saul's Sin and Rejection (1 Sam. 13; 15)

Before Saul was made king, Samuel had given his approval to the demand for a king (1 Sam. 10:24; 12:1) and had promised to support Saul, with the definite understanding that the new king would recognize always his dependence upon God and would be obedient to the will of God as revealed to him by the prophet Samuel. As we have seen, at first Saul kept his word. The secret of his tragic failure at the end was his refusal to be obedient to God. It is worthy of note that in every instance the prophet kept his word and always proved his integrity in his dealings with Saul.

After two years of reign, the wilful and rebellious spirit of Saul was beginning to assert itself. His first sin was in his failure to wait for Samuel before going to battle and in his assuming the role of the prophet. For this Samuel sternly rebuked Saul and told him that ultimately the kingdom would be taken from his family (1 Sam. 13:8–14).

The occasion for Saul's second sin, which proved decisive, soon presented itself (1 Sam. 15). After successfully defeating Moab, Ammon, and Edom, Saul received from Samuel the command that he should go to war against the Amalekites, their bitter and cruel enemy in the south. He was to administer decisive defeat upon them. Saul went as commanded and was completely victorious in the campaign. He carried out the instructions to the letter, except for sparing the life of Agag the king, and saving the best of the cattle. Saul lied to the prophet, professing to have carried out his order in detail. It was necessary now for Samuel to pronounce the doom awaiting the disobedient and deceptive

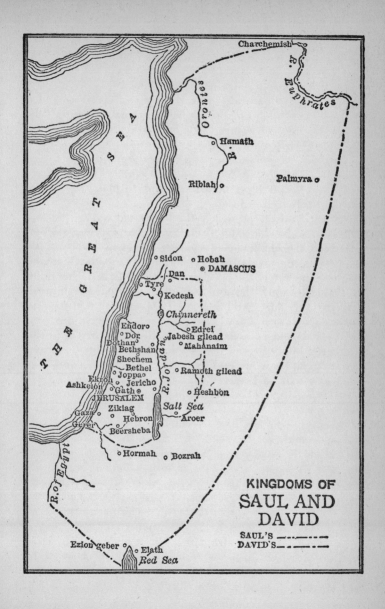

KINGDOMS OF
**SAUL AND
DAVID**

SAUL'S ------
DAVID'S ------

king: "Because thou hast rejected the word of Jehovah, he hath also rejected thee from being king" (1 Sam. 15:23 ASV). Another account tells of Samuel's secret anointing of David in Bethlehem, as the future king (1 Sam. 16:1–13).

His rejection naturally proved to be a disastrous blow to Saul. Even though he was allowed to remain king until his death, his last years were tragic ones. His mind was affected by some sort of madness. His judgment and actions were no longer normal. Periods of deep depression and gloom came upon him. To restore him to sanity, a youthful musician, the boy David, was brought to the court to play the harp to soothe Saul's frenzied soul.

At first Saul's treatment of the lad David was cordial and friendly. Somewhat later David, with the approval of Saul, accepted the challenge of Goliath the giant leader of the Philistines. By his dramatic victory over Goliath, David became immediately the popular hero to all Israel. This praise of David inflamed the soul of Saul, and he became insanely jealous of the lad. "And Saul eyed David from that day and forward" (1 Sam. 18:9). Despite the unjustified treatment by Saul, David behaved like a gentleman and still further endeared himself to all the people. "David behaved himself wisely in all his ways; and Jehovah was with him. And when Saul saw that he behaved himself very wisely, he stood in awe of him. But all Israel and Judah loved David; for he went out and came in before them" (1 Sam. 18:14–16 ASV).

Seemingly during the time when Saul was chasing David, the aged and honored Samuel came to the end of his days. All Israel came together and buried him in his home at Ramah, the scene of so many historic events in his life. His had been a long and distinguished career. He had guided his people in the crucial years of establishing the kingdom. By his unimpeachable integrity, his unwavering loyalty to Jehovah, his wise counsel, and his sound judgment he had made a contribution to his nation which few have surpassed. His influence was more widespread than that of any judge who preceded him. Samuel may be classed as judge, prophet, priest, statesman, and kingmaker.

4. The Death of Saul (1 Sam. 31)

The unhappy plight of Saul grew steadily worse until it culminated in his tragic death on Mount Gilboa. These closing years witnessed a rapid decline in his service to his people and in his own personal fortunes. The Philistines, sensing the desperate situation in Israel, came again with a great army for the knockout blow. David was a refugee in Philistia, but did not join with them in the war against Saul. With a small army, poorly organized and greatly discouraged, the king must face the mighty hosts of the Philistines. He was in desperate straits.

The battle took place next day on Mount Gilboa. The meager and discouraged army of Saul was soon put to rout. The Philistines pursued Saul and his sons and killed three of these, including Jonathan. When his armor-bearer refused to kill him, the wounded king fell upon his own sword and died in the midst of his enemies.

5. Evaluation of Saul's Career

Thus ended the life of the first king of Israel, a career which began well and might have closed in glory. His great weakness was his spirit of rebellion and self-will. He used his power to forward his tyrannical purposes. Resisting steadily the Spirit of God, he reaped the bitter fruits of his own folly.

However, he rendered a distinct service to his people and, perhaps unconsciously, laid some foundations that made possible the brilliant achievements of David his successor.

To the end, David recognized Saul as "the Lord's anointed" (2 Sam. 1:14). David's lament over Saul helps us to realize that there must have been strength as well as weakness in the leadership of Israel's first king.

> Thy glory, O Israel, is slain upon thy high places!
> How are the mighty fallen!
> Ye daughters of Israel, weep over Saul,
> Who clothed you in scarlet delicately,
> Who put ornaments of gold upon your apparel.
> > 2 Samuel 1:19, 24 ASV

III. DAVID, ISRAEL'S GREATEST KING (1 Sam. 19–31; 2 Sam.
1–24; 1 Kings 1–2; 1 Chron. 10–29)

We turn now to the career of David, the greatest of all the
kings of Israel. He came from the large and important tribe
of Judah, which occupied a most significant place in the
history of the Hebrew people. He was the son of Jesse, who
was a pious and prominent descendant of Ruth and Boaz.

1. *His Early Years* (1 Sam. 16–17)

David was born in Bethlehem, a little city six miles south
of Jerusalem. He was a shepherd lad. As such he developed
self-reliance, courage, and a meditative spirit. From the first
he seems to have been devout and worshipful in spirit. He
was clean in his habits and is described as attractive in appearance with a ruddy complexion. He must have had an
unusual combination of desirable qualities—modesty, sincerity, warmth, piety, faith, courage, and a brilliant mind.

We have already noted Saul's insane jealousy of David,
which made it necessary for the future king to flee from
Saul for a long time. This unhappy experience ended when
the fugitive was received as a refugee in Ziklag of Philistia.
It was during David's stay in Philistia that Saul died on
Mount Gilboa. Upon receiving this news, David composed
a beautiful tribute to Saul and Jonathan.

2. *David Becomes King* (2 Sam. 1–5; 1 Chron. 11–12)

The death of Saul left the Israelites without a king. After
praying to God, David was told to go to Hebron, where the
leaders of Judah would make him their king. In this ancient
city, so prominent in the lives of his forefathers, David set
up his kingdom and for seven and one half years ruled over
Judah.

After the death of Saul, only one son, Ishbosheth, survived. Under the leadership of Abner, a very influential military figure in Saul's regimé, Ishbosheth was made king of all
the tribes except Judah. He set up his kingdom at Mahanaim,
a city east of the Jordan. Abner later turned against Ish-

bosheth and succeeded in convincing all the tribes to unite, with David as king. In the meantime Ishbosheth was murdered in bed.

When representatives appeared before David offering him kingship over all Israel, he accepted and was publicly anointed. At last, after years of trial and disappointment, he was the official ruler of the entire nation. He was the people's choice; he had their hearty support and was now ready to begin a reign which was destined to be a most glorious one.

One of David's first undertakings was to capture the old fortress of Jebus and make this his capital city. In this way Jerusalem was to become the most famous city in history.

Having secured his capital, David planned to make it headquarters for the religious life of the nation also. When the ark of the covenant was safely deposited in its new home, special sacrifices were offered and the multitude returned to their homes (2 Sam. 6:1-19).

It was the sincere desire of David to build a glorious temple for the worship of Jehovah. However, it was revealed to him that this honor should not be his because he was a man of war, but that it would be reserved for his son as a man of peace. Even though Solomon was to build the Temple, David made all preparations for it, including the actual plans of the building. Shortly afterwards God sent Nathan, his prophet, to the king with a special message indicating God's pleasure in David and promising to prosper his reign and to make him great among men.

3. *David's Conquests* (2 Sam. 8:1-13; 1 Chron. 18)

David now inaugurated a series of campaigns for the conquest of the surrounding nations, in which he was eminently successful. The record of these significant conquests is a very brief one but the effects were far-reaching, including: (1) the subjugation of the Philistines, (2) the conquest of Moab, (3) the defeat of Hadadezer of Zobath, (4) the subduing of Edom, and (5) finally, conquering the Ammonites and the Syrians.

With the completion of these conquests, David had secured dominion over a vast territory extending from the Euphrates to Egypt, a kingdom some fifty thousand square miles in area. At no other time did the Hebrew kingdom attain such an extended area. Having established his kingdom, David now set up the organization for his government. While he as king was at the head, he selected a cabinet and several advisors who should work with him in the administration of governmental affairs.

4. David's Great Sin (2 Sam. 11–12)

When the king was at the height of his power and fame, he fell victim to temptation and, in an hour of weakness, committed a gross sin which brought shame and fearful consequences to himself and his family. He became infatuated with a beautiful woman, Bathsheba, the wife of Uriah, one of his soldiers on duty with the army. His sin of adultery with her illustrates the common weakness of man. Realizing his difficulty, the king ordered Joab to arrange for the death of Uriah by having him placed in the front ranks in battle, where death would be certain. This done, David then took Bathsheba as his wife.

But such behavior was not to pass unnoticed. God sent his faithful prophet Nathan, who previously had brought God's message of approval to David, to rebuke the king for his sin. This man of God tactfully presented the matter by the use of a story (2 Sam. 12:1–14). Nathan then proceeded to point out the enormity of David's sin and to announce the penalty that God would impose. In true humility the great king confessed his guilt, declared his willingness to suffer, and then prayed for God's forgiveness (Psalm 51).

The effect of transgression is never confined to the life of the guilty party. The consequences of David's wrongdoing were tragically reflected in the life of the royal family for years to come. Domestic troubles came thick and fast. The seed which the king had sown bore a harvest of shame in the lives of his own family. His son Amnon became infatuated with Tamar, his half sister, and forced her in the sin of fornication. Her brother Absalom avenged her disgrace by killing Amnon (2 Sam. 13).

David's son Absalom now launched a rebellion against him and took over the government for a brief time. David was forced to flee from Jerusalem. His army rallied to his support, and in a battle with the army of Absalom the rebellion was crushed and Absalom was killed (2 Sam. 15–18). As David was returning to Jerusalem to take up again the kingship, another rebellion led by Sheba broke out. This too was soon crushed. David made a heroic effort to "come back" but his advanced age and other difficulties made it impossible for him to regain fully the prestige and power which he had formerly enjoyed.

5. *His Closing Years* (1 Kings 1–2; 1 Chron. 22–29)

The close of the reign of David came rapidly. Not long before the end he summoned his son Solomon and gave over to him all the supplies which had been gathered for building the Temple, including even the detail plans for its arrangement and construction. By this act David showed his preference as to his successor.

Adonijah, one of David's sons, made an unsuccessful attempt to become king, but when Solomon was formally acclaimed, Adonijah pledged his allegiance.

Shortly after this David, the honored and beloved king, was gathered to his fathers, having reigned forty years. He was buried on Mount Zion, in the city which he had made famous. Thus ended the career of Israel's greatest ruler.

David was probably the most colorful character in Hebrew history. He occupies a place of greatness next to Moses in all of the Old Testament. And there are good reasons for his great name. He had many excellent qualities and was one of the most versatile of men.

IV. SOLOMON, THE KING OF NATIONAL SPLENDOR (1 Kings 1–11; 2 Chron. 1–9)

Solomon, the new king, was the son of David and Bathsheba. While we know but little of the experiences of his early life, we may assume that as the son of the king he would have exceptional advantages and that he probably made good use of these opportunities. He had a good mind and certainly in the beginning of his reign was a man of sincere purpose and of a religious spirit.

1. *His Auspicious Start* (2 Chron. 1)

Solomon assumed direction of the nation at the time of its greatest material prosperity and splendor. His kingdom, extending from Mesopotamia to Egypt, comprised some fifty thousand square miles of territory—the largest in its history. The people were united and at peace with one another and with surrounding nations. David had left a remarkable heritage to his son.

Early in his reign, Solomon, with a large assembly, went to Gibeon, six miles north of Jerusalem for the offering of sacrifices. At night Jehovah appeared to the king and said, "Ask what I shall give thee." The young king, as yet humble in heart, asked not for riches or long life or honor or for the death of his enemies, but for an understanding heart to judge the people and to discriminate between good and evil. This pleased Jehovah, who promised Solomon not only what he had asked, but in addition to these both riches and honor.

It is traditional to think of Solomon as an exceptionally wise man. Unquestionably he had a remarkable knowledge of the natural world, plants, and animals, as his proverbs demonstrate. He seems also to have had a deep understanding of human nature. He was a keen observer of human life and knew well the folly of sin and wickedness and the wisdom of prudence and virtue. However, a careful examination of his entire career leads one to question his wisdom, certainly in his behavior. The latter years of his life witness the violation of many of the principles of wisdom which he so eloquently proclaimed.

2. *His Building Enterprises* (2 Chron. 2–8)

One of the first big undertakings of Solomon was to erect the Temple which David had planned and had instructed him to build. This venture was an enormous one, involving much planning, securing materials, and providing workmen. The building was famous, becoming "the joy of all the earth," not because of its size, since it was comparatively small, but because of its magnificence and the quality of its materials. It was finished only after seven long years of work.

At last, when the building was completed, an elaborate program of dedication was observed. All twelve tribes were invited. The king, elevated in a chair of brass, presided over the ceremonies. The ark was brought in and placed in the holy of holies, as a cloud filled the house to hide the presence of Jehovah. The dedication lasted seven days and was then followed by the Feast of Tabernacles, which was lengthened to two weeks instead of the usual one week.

After the completion of the Temple, Solomon set about the construction of a series of buildings, which has been called the "Palace Complex." This was an elaborate palace for himself, which consisted of some five structures and required thirteen years for its completion. Solomon also built a palace for his queen, the daughter of Pharaoh (1 Kings 7:1-12).

Not all Solomon's building enterprises were in Jerusalem. To carry on effectively his vast trade enterprises, he built up many store cities. It is impossible to say how much wealth came into Solomon's hands through his commercial activities. One scholar has estimated the yearly total at more than one hundred million dollars. We can be certain that it was stupendous. The accumulation of such wealth, together with the luxurious life of the court resulting from it, brought about a deplorable condition in his kingdom.

3. *The Mistakes of Solomon* (1 Kings 11)

The years of Solomon's reign brought a change, not only in the character of his government, but also in the ideals and the conduct of the king himself. Toward the end he had lost his spirit of modesty and humility and had become conceited, haughty, and despotic. Riches and luxury had enslaved him and left him restless and unsatisfied. Surrounded by untold wealth and acclaimed as the world's wisest man, he came to the end of his days a pathetic figure.

The great sin of Solomon was his loss of devotion to Jehovah. He brought into his court many wives and concubines from Egypt, Moab, Ammon, and many other lands. For them he sought to provide the facilities for the practice of their pagan religious rites, which meant the worship of their idols. The result was the making of Jerusalem the scene of worship of pagan idols and heathen gods. This was the sin that proved fatal to Solomon.

Some years before the death of Solomon, the outlines of failure and disaster could be discerned. His own people, weary of the heavy burden of taxes for the support of his luxurious court, grew restless and finally rebellious. The surrounding nations that had been oppressed for so long began to gather their forces for rebellion. The kingdom, while appearing outwardly as unified and strong, was, in reality, honeycombed with weaknesses that were to issue in the fatal division soon after Solomon's death.

After a reign of forty years "Solomon slept with his fathers, and was buried in the city of David his father" (1 Kings 11:43). In many respects his character is a puzzle. There were many noble qualities in his make-up, particularly in his early years. To be sure he was swept off his feet by wealth, luxury, and fame, but there is no intimation of a lack of honor or integrity in his life. Unquestionably he was a far better man than the ordinary Oriental ruler of his time. We could only wish that he had been strong enough to withstand the temptations that came to him.

V. Summary of the Period

This period of Bible history, which covers less than two hundred years, was marked by military conquest, brilliant achievements, and unparalleled wealth and splendor. The first kings of Israel were held in veneration by Jewish people for many centuries afterward. They pointed back to this period as their golden age, and continued to dream of another such era, which never came.

Material splendor and wealth, which they sought and obtained, brought apostasy and ruin. The people had to learn that greatness as a nation is not measured by material things. A nation, like an individual, has a character, either good or bad, weak or strong. The fundamental virtues are as essential in national life as in personal living. The common vices will wreck a nation as well as a man.

The leading figures were Samuel, Saul, David, and Solomon. The biblical record contains no mention of any serious sin of Samuel—except for his failure with his own sons (1 Sam. 8:3)—but it speaks freely of the sins of Saul, David, and Solomon. The very fact that the Bible tells fully and frankly of the mistakes or sins of these men is significant. They were national heroes and yet their sins are recorded in detail. This record offers convincing proof that sin is universal. No class or rank is exempt. Sin is the foe of all men. We may notice also that sin always brings suffering and often tragedy. Saul's rebellion against Jehovah brought his downfall. David's inexcusable sin brought tragedy in his own life, and in that of his family. Solomon's reign closed in the shadows because of his forsaking the God whom he had sworn to serve with unwavering loyalty. The biblical record of these years in the kingdom of Israel has great significance for men in every age.

FOR CLASS DISCUSSION AND FURTHER STUDY

1. Continue to trace the development of the people whom God meant to be his witnesses and through whom the Redeemer was to come. Discuss—
   (1) How Samuel restored the worship of Jehovah
   (2) The preservation of the records of the line from which Messiah was to come (the Old Testament genealogies)
   (3) How Saul, David, and Solomon were used in bringing national unity and prestige to the Chosen People
2. What was the sin that led to Saul's rejection? Compare Saul's sin was David's great sin. Which seems to be the blacker and more immoral? Why then, was Saul rejected while David was honored by God and chosen to be an ancestor of Jesus

Christ? In your study of this problem consider Psalms 51 and 32.

3. Secure or make a map showing the area covered by the kingdom of David and of Solomon. Color the map to show the area of the kingdom at its maximum extent.

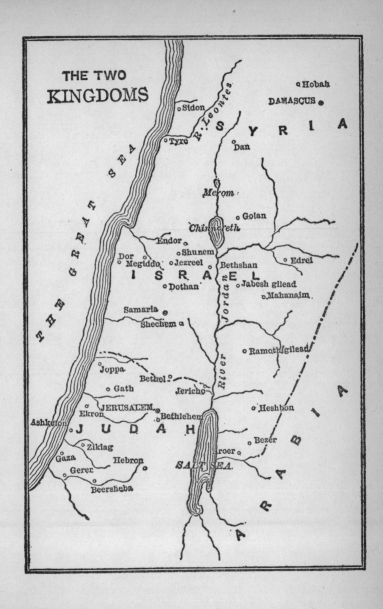

CHAPTER 5

I. THE DIVISION OF THE KINGDOM (1 Kings 12)

II. THE KINGDOM OF ISRAEL (1 Kings 12 to 2 Kings 17)
1. The Rulers of Israel
2. The Fatal Policy of Jeroboam
3. Omri and Ahab
4. Jeroboam II
5. Drifting Toward Destruction

III. THE KINGDOM OF JUDAH (1 Kings 11–25; 2 Kings 1–23; and 2 Chron. 10–36)
1. The Rulers of Judah
2. Rehoboam's Folly
3. Asa and Jehoshaphat
4. Hezekiah and Josiah

IV. THE BABYLONIAN CAPTIVITY (2 Kings 24–25)
1. Babylonian Conquests
2. The Fall of Judah
3. Taken into Captivity

5

The Period of the Rival Kingdoms

WITH THE DEATH of Solomon, far-reaching events took place. The ten Northern tribes, under the leadership of Jeroboam, seceded and formed a new nation called the Northern Kingdom, or Israel. Judah continued its existence as a nation contemporary with Israel.

The period we now study covers a long stretch of years. It opened with the split of the kingdom left by Solomon, around 950 B.C. and closed with the captivity of Judah 587–586 B.C. The biblical record of this period is found in the books of Kings, Chronicles, and in the historical sections in some of the books of prophecy. The rupture which resulted in two rival kingdoms is told in detail. The main story of these two kingdoms is woven into one account, giving now the main developments in one and shifting quickly to outstanding occurrences in the other. The story includes the downfall of Israel with the capture of Samaria in 722 B.C. From this point the Bible historian deals with the experiences of Judah alone, not mentioning Israel again, until Jerusalem is captured and the last group of exiles is taken to Babylonia in 587–586 B.C. Naturally, the record centers around the actions of the nineteen kings in Israel and the nineteen kings and one queen in Judah.

I. THE DIVISION OF THE KINGDOM (1 Kings 12)

The causes of the schism were both indirect and direct. Indirectly the causes go back for some time. For many years there had been keen rivalry between the strong tribe of Judah in the south, with its capital city of Jerusalem, and some of the tribes further north. We have seen this showing up in at least two instances. After the death of Saul, the

Northern tribes did not immediately accept David as king, even though he had been anointed by Samuel. They formed their own kingdom with Ishbosheth as king. Again after the rebellion of Absalom had been crushed, Sheba started a new revolt with the cry that David was not fair to them.

The direct cause of the division was the foolish behavior of Rehoboam, who succeeded Solomon. When Rehoboam went up to Shechem for the confirmation of his coronation, the Northern tribes under Jeroboam vigorously demanded a statement from the new king as to his policy. They were tired of heavy taxes and tyrranical treatment by their king. Rehoboam wisely asked for time to prepare an answer. Three days were allowed for this. During this time the king sought advice from two groups. The older and wiser men urged him to be cautious and considerate, warning him of the real peril. The younger men, probably his friends in the court, advised that he treat the people harshly and "put them in their place" at once by a bold threat.

Rehoboam foolishly heeded the advice of the younger men and in his reply to the Northern tribes made a harsh threatening speech. The reaction was immediate. Contrary to what Rehoboam probably expected, they shouted defiantly, "What portion have we in David? neither have we inheritance in the son of Jesse: to your tents, O Israel: now see to thine own house, David" (1 Kings 12:16). The die was cast. The kingdom was split. Jeroboam set to work at once, and the new kingdom became a reality.

Judah and Israel existed as rival nations for about 250 years, that is until Israel was conquered by Assyria in 722 B.C. Since it will be simpler and easier to discuss the history of each kingdom separately, we shall deal first with Israel as a nation from the time of its founding until its conquest. We shall then go back to trace the main events in the history of Judah until it was conquered by Babylonia in 587 B.C.

II. THE KINGDOM OF ISRAEL (1 Kings 12 to 2 Kings 17)

The biblical record gives the names of nineteen men who served as kings over the Northern Kingdom. The list of

these men, with the number of years each served, is as
follows:

1. *The Rulers of Israel*

As you consider the number of rulers, note the evidences of
frequent changes in government.

Jeroboam I	22 years	Jehoahaz	17 years
Nadab	2 years	Jehoash	16 years
Baasha	24 years	Jeroboam II	41 years
Elah	2 years	Zachariah	6 months
Zimri	7 days	Shallum	1 month
Omri	12 years	Menahem	10 years
Ahab	22 years	Pekahiah	2 years
Ahaziah	2 years	Pekah	20 years
Jehoram	12 years	Hoshea	9 years
Jehu	28 years		

Since it is impossible to relate the experiences of each of
these kings, we shall select only the most important in the
effort to keep in the main current of the history.

2. *The Fatal Policy of Jeroboam* (1 Kings 12:25 to 14:21)

Jeroboam, first king, had to "start from scratch," since he
had no capital city, no treasury, no cabinet, and no kind of
organization. He selected Shechem, prominent in the affairs
of the people for several centuries, as the seat of his new
government.

Jeroboam faced a real problem in the deeply intrenched
practice of his people in going to the city of Jerusalem for
the various religious ceremonies demanded of them. To
meet the situation, Jeroboam set up two shrines for worship
in his own territory, one at Bethel, only a short distance from
his southern boundary, and one at Dan in the far north. The
tragic mistake of Jeroboam was in the nature of the worship
which he instituted in these places. Instead of Jehovah worship, it was idolatry. At these places he set up two calves of
gold, around which all worship was to center. In this fatal
policy Jeroboam set the standard for his government. Each
succeeding king followed this policy, which led ultimately

to the downfall of the kingdom. Idolatry was never completely exterminated. Later the worship of Baal with all its
horrible practices found a welcome and congenial soil in
this kingdom.

Jeroboam was an able ruler showing great strength in
organization and leadership. He made Israel a real nation.
However, his zeal in promoting idolatry earned for him
the title, "Jeroboam, the son of Nebat, who made Israel to
sin." This designation is used about twenty times in 1 and 2
Kings.

3. Omri and Ahab (1 Kings 16:16 to 22:40)

Omri, who came some twenty-five years later, was also
an able king. The biblical record of his work is very brief.
His chief achievement, in this record, was the setting up of a
new capital city, to which he gave the name Samaria. This
city was destined to become famous in Israel's history. The
reign of Omri is significant because of his relationship with
foreign powers, even though this is not mentioned in the
biblical account. He was known as a powerful and influential
ruler by the Assyrian people. He established trade relations
with a number of nations, including Phoenicia and Moab. It
should be recorded that the policy of Omri in religious matters was to walk in the path of Jeroboam and all other kings
of Israel; in fact, the record states that he "did worse than
all that were before him" (1 Kings 16:25).

The reign of Ahab was one of the most eventful and ob-
jectionable of all kings. He was a weakling who was dominated by his wicked wife Jezebel, whose consuming ambition
was to destroy the worship of Jehovah in Israel and to make
the worship of Baal universal. The biblical record of the evil
deeds of Jezebel and Ahab presents a dark picture. The
career of the evil king ended with his death in a battle with
Benhadad of Syria. A few years later Jezebel was murdered
by Jehu, who came to be king of Israel.

In the midst of the reign of Ahab, the dynamic prophet
Elijah appeared suddenly to challenge the wicked design.
The three years drought and the contest on Mount Carmel

with the death of the prophets of Baal and the enheartening of the followers of Jehovah all took place in this reign. Elijah's great contribution was in saving Israel from complete envelopment by Baalism. Elijah was succeeded by the gentle but powerful Elisha, who had a long and notable ministry in Israel.

The end of the house of Ahab and Jezebel was brought about by the murder of all their descendants by Jehu. However, the reign of Jehu may be considered a total failure so far as any constructive achievements are concerned.

4. Jeroboam II (2 Kings 14:23-29)

The next king of Israel whose accomplishments were of any significance was Jeroboam II, who began his work some 150 years after the kingdom was founded. He had a long reign of 41 years in which he did much to make Israel a great and prosperous nation. This tide of material prosperity brought serious decline in moral and religious life. During this time the two famous prophets, Amos and Hosea, did all they could to save the nation, but they were unable to stem the tide of materialism and rebellion against Jehovah. At the death of Jeroboam II, any close observer could see that the end of the kingdom could not be far off.

5. Drifting Toward Destruction (2 Kings 15-17)

We now study an era of anarchy and bloodshed when "the dagger was the symbol of the immediate future." The religious apostasy and moral collapse resulting from the prosperity under Jeroboam II had weakened the nation and destroyed the moral fiber of the people. Henceforth, even to the end of the kingdom (722 B.C.), it was an era of revolution and murder. In the last fifty years there were five different ruling families on the throne, most of whom came to the throne by revolt and assassination. It was indeed a time when, as the prophet declared, "blood toucheth blood" (Hos. 4:2).

During these last fifty years a great empire was rising like a black cloud in the east. Assyria had at this time a number of able and aggressive kings. These kings, understanding the weaknesses of Syria, Israel, and Judah, began to plan the conquest of western Asia so that they would be in an advantageous position against Egypt.

In 732 B.C. Tiglath-pileser (called Tilgath-pilneser in 1 Chron. 5:6, 26; 2 Chron. 28:20) conquered Damascus. Ten years later, 722 B.C., Israel was conquered when Samaria fell to Sargon II. Thus ended the kingdom of Israel, founded in revolt over two hundred years earlier. Those captured and taken unto Assyria—a small number for what was once a populous kingdom—are not mentioned again in the record.

The two hundred and fifty years of history covered by the Northern Kingdom was a period of great importance, particularly in religious life. The great social, political, and religious problems in Israel brought forth some of the greatest prophets and teachers of all Hebrew history. The ministries of Elijah, Elisha, Jonah, Amos, and Hosea—all in this period—gave to the world a rich heritage of truth needed for the social and religious problems of each generation. Their messages are both timely and timeless. Indeed, we may say that the failure of this Northern Kingdom to produce an abiding material kingdom was a small matter compared to the fine contribution made by her prophets. It is ironical that the very wickedness of its people should be the means of calling forth prophets whose condemnation of the sins of their own people should constitute the chief glory and contribution of the kingdom. (See chapter 7.)

III. THE KINGDOM OF JUDAH (1 Kings 11–25; 2 Kings 1–23; 2 Chron. 10–36)

We shall go back now to the time of the division of the kingdom and trace the main outlines of the history of the Southern Kingdom after the ten Northern tribes seceded. In some respects Judah had the advantage over Israel. The people of the Southern Kingdom had the city of Jerusalem, dear to every Jew, as their capital. They were bound together by strong bonds, national ideals, and social interests. The centralized worship in the Temple was a source of national unity. Furthermore, all the kings of Judah were descendants of David, their great hero.

1. *The Rulers of Judah*

There were nineteen kings and one queen during this period of some four hundred years, as follows:

Rehoboam	17 years	Jotham	16 years
Abijah	3 years	Ahaz	16 years
Asa	41 years	Hezekiah	29 years
Jehoshaphat	25 years	Manasseh	55 years
Jehoram	8 years	Amon	2 years
Ahaziah	1 year	Josiah	31 years
Athaliah (queen)	6 years	Jehoahaz	3 months
Joash	40 years	Jehoiakim	11 years
Amaziah	29 years	Jehoiachin	3 months
Uzziah	52 years	Zedekiah	11 years

We shall limit our discussion to the reigns of several of the more significant kings.

2. *Rehoboam's Folly* (1 Kings 11:41 to 14:31; 2 Chron. 10–12)

Rehoboam's suicidal policy in losing the ten Northern tribes left him in a greatly weakened condition. Realizing too late what had occurred, he made desperate efforts over a period of several years to regain control over these revolting tribes. At the beginning Rehoboam apparently tried to walk in the ways of Jehovah. Before long, however, he fell into the same sins as his father Solomon. He took a number of wives and concubines and set up altars to their gods in his kingdom (2 Chron. 11:18 to 12:1).

3. *Asa and Jehoshaphat* (1 Kings 15:8–24; 22:41–50; 2 Chron. 14:1 to 21:1)

Asa, the grandson of Rehoboam, deserved the designation "good" since from the very first he began his program of destroying idolatry and re-establishing the worship of Jehovah in his realm. He expelled the Sodomites and destroyed the idols erected before his time. Asa proved to be an able warrior and statesman also. He fortified many cities in his territory, and his standing army was numbered at 580,000 men.

The latter years of his reign seem to have been marked by a general breakdown of his faith in God. He died after a long reign of forty-one years which, taken as a whole, was a good administration. He was buried with great mourning by his people in Jerusalem.

Jehoshaphat, the son of Asa, ruled over Judah twenty-five years. He was an able king, both as a statesman and a religious leader. Indeed, he is rated as one of the best of all Judah's kings. He was vitally interested in the worship of his people and showed his interest early in his reign by a nation-wide program of teaching the people.

He built up a very large army, more than one million men, under competent officers. He fortified a number of cities in Judah and Ephraim. He restored many of the offices of government created by David. His reign was one of genuine prosperity.

Some years after Jehoshaphat, Athaliah, the daughter of Ahab and Jezebel, usurped the throne and ruled for six years, until the boy Joash was proclaimed king, at which time Athaliah was murdered. The reign of Joash was comparatively insignificant, as was that of his son Amaziah. Then came the long reign of Uzziah (52 years). He was an able ruler and at first was loyal to Jehovah, though his last years were marked by apostasy.

4. *Hezekiah and Josiah* (2 Kings 18–20; 22–23; 2 Chron. 29–32; 34–35)

One of the ablest and most faithful of all Judah's kings was Hezekiah, who was in power at the time of the great Assyrian invasions when Israel was finally destroyed. He began his reign by instituting a vigorous reformation in worship. He was also a great builder and organizer. During his reign Jerusalem (and Judah) were miraculously saved from conquest by Sennacherib, the Assyrian king, when his army was mysteriously destroyed. Had it not been for this miracle,

out walls for protection, was left in complete ruin. For more than a century it was to remain a desolation.

3. *Taken into Captivity* (2 Kings 25:18-21; 2 Chron. 36:9-21)

When the work of destruction had been completed, the best of the remaining people were taken away as captives. This was the third and last group from Judah to go to their new home in exile. It will be seen that the captivity was in reality not an event, but a process. Three different groups were taken away in the years 605, 597, and 587-586 B.C. The kingdom of Judah was at an end!

Only a small remnant of poor, discouraged, and leaderless people was now left in Judah. To control them Nebuchadnezzar appointed a man named Gedaliah as governor. His headquarters were at Mizpah, a little town a few miles north of Jerusalem. Jeremiah remained in Judah to do what he could to encourage this desolate remnant. He was the only steadying influence left. To the groups who went away into captivity he offered encouragement and hope. He boldly predicted that some day they would return to their homeland. Such a hope seemed so impossible and preposterous that few, if any, dared believe it.

It appears that insurrection soon broke out among those left in Judah. Gedaliah was murdered by Ishmael, a member of the royal family, and civil war resulted. Fearing the wrath of Nebuchadnezzar, the leaders fled to Egypt and took Jeremiah with them. What Nebuchadnezzar did about this is not known.

In this unhappy manner the once-glorious Hebrew kingdom ended. According to the biblical record this was caused by the failure of the people to be loyal to Jehovah their God. Their persistent policy of rebellion and wickedness resulted in this experience so filled with sorrow and humiliation.

We have to use imagination to understand the feeling of despair which must have possessed most of the people who were now the captives of Babylonia. And yet the situation was not altogether hopeless. Jeremiah, the faithful prophet, had done much to prepare them for this disaster. He had advised them to accept their situation and go on to Babylon. He had also assured them that some of them would later return and the nation would continue to live. He was with them now as they made ready to go away. He did not go with them, but he did give hope and encouragement by letter after they reached their new home. Ezekiel also brought comfort to them by his presence and his messages while in exile. Certainly there were some devout and hopeful people who did not surrender to hopelessness. Even though it was dark, they could recount similar experiences in their history when God had been their helper.

The story of the rise and decline of kingdoms has been repeated many times. History has a way of repeating itself. It is good to know history; it is much better to learn the lessons of history. The causes of the downfall of nations are usually the same in any century. The sins which brought ruin to Judah have been repeated in the case of many other kingdoms. What happened to the once-glorious kingdom of David and Solomon may happen to any nation today.

Israel was God's chosen nation, and this was not the closing chapter in their history. They were to experience long, hard years of shame and suffering, but out of this was to come a wiser and better nation which would better serve God's purpose for them.

FOR CLASS DISCUSSION AND FURTHER STUDY

1. As you continue to trace the unfolding story of God's plan of redemption, consider—
    (1) The failure of the Chosen People to maintain a clear witness for the Lord
    (2) Why God had to purge the nation he had chosen to be his instrument for carrying his message to the world
2. Copy the charts of the kings of Israel and Judah as they appear in this chapter. From chapter 7 discover the names of prophets

who prophesied in Israel and list each prophet's name opposite
the name of the king, or kings, in whose reign he prophesied.
Do the same for the prophets of Judah. Hold your completed
charts for further use with chapter 7.

CHAPTER 6

I. THE YEARS OF EXILE (Jer., Ezek., Dan., Esther)
  1. A New World for the Jews
  2. The Nature of the Exile
  3. Benefits Derived from the Exile

II. THE RESTORATION (2 Chron. 36:22–23; Ezra; Neh.; Hag.; Mal.)
  1. The Decree of Cyrus
  2. Zerubbabel and His Company
  3. Ezra Returns to Jerusalem
  4. The Contribution of Nehemiah

III. THE INTERBIBLICAL PERIOD
  1. A Period of Significant Changes
  2. The Jews Under Persian Rule
  3. The Conquest of the Greeks
  4. Hebrew Independence
  5. The Conquest by the Romans
  6. Preparation for the Advent of Jesus Christ

6

The Years of Suffering and Silence

THE PERIOD which we are now to study begins with the fall of Jerusalem 587–586 B.C. and it goes to the opening of the New Testament. For the Jews it was a time, not only of humiliation and sorrow, but of radical changes in nearly every area of their lives.

This seemingly crushed and hopeless little group was to go on living. The great Babylonian empire, which was wielding such power, would ultimately fall. The proud Persians, who were soon to crush Babylon, would flourish for a while and then pass into oblivion. The kingdoms of Greece and Rome, too, would pass off the scene. But the little remnant of Jewish people would not be destroyed.

I. THE YEARS OF EXILE (Jer., Ezek., Dan., Esther)

We have already noted that there were three different importations of these exiles into Babylonia (605, 597–596, 587–586 B.C.). The total number cannot be finally determined with accuracy. Probably the most frequent estimate of 50,000 is not far wrong. They represented the leading people from every point of view.

1. A New World for the Jews

What kind of a world was this new home of theirs? Compared to the poor little country of Palestine it was a big, rich, and prosperous country. Here the Jews found an advanced culture, big business, and materialistic splendor. Babylon, the chief city, was one of great wealth and magnificence. It was the center of a vast empire, including all of Mesopotamia and the highlands beyond, as well as Syria and Palestine.

This kingdom was famous also for the advanced stage of culture and learning which its people had attained. The Magi were learned men of Babylonia, with a wide reputation for wisdom. The people were skilled in astronomy and astrology. They had libraries and a well-developed literature. They were advanced in the art of making pottery and in textile work. In such a wealthy, cultured, and prosperous kingdom the captive Jews were to make their home.

2. *The Nature of the Exile*

The Jewish exiles were placed in a rich plain on the river or canal, Chebar, which connected Babylon with Nippur (Ezek. 1:1–3). Apparently they enjoyed great freedom in this new home, even though they appear to have been segregated. It should be noted that they were not slaves, ill-treated and forced to do unbearable work like their forefathers in Egypt. They were colonists with freedom to do practically as they chose, provided of course, that they were loyal to the Babylonian Government. That some of the Jews attained positions or prominence at various times and under various rules during the exile is seen in the accounts of Daniel and his friends and (at a later date) of Esther and Mordecai.

One may ask then, in view of all the advantages the exiles enjoyed in their new home, if there was any punishment in this period of exile. How did the Jews themselves feel about it all? Unquestionably there was homesickness, resentment, and bitterness toward their captors. The disgrace of the captivity was in the loss of their freedom, in the destruction of their government, and in being a people without a country. They were subjects of another power, a strange people in a strange land.

According to Jeremiah's prediction, they were to return after seventy years (Jer. 25:11). The time from the captivity of the first group, 607–606 B.C., to the time of the return of the first group, 536 B.C., would make seventy years. Also the time from the destruction of Jerusalem, 586 B.C., and the taking of the last group of exiles, to the time of the completion of the rebuilt Temple, 516 B.C., would make seventy years.

The years of exile produced a twofold crisis for the Jews in their religious life. Amidst the prosperity of Babylonia with all its attractive opportunities for material gain, many were tempted to drift away from the faith of their fathers. The many who genuinely desired to be loyal to their God also had a problem. Among all peoples of their day, gods were thought of as tribal or national. No doubt many Hebrew people thought of Jehovah as a national God who could be worshiped only in Palestine. "How shall we sing the Lord's song in a strange land?" they asked (Psalm 137:4). Through Ezekiel and other prophets and teachers, they had to learn that Jehovah their God could be worshiped anywhere. He is near to all, the God whose presence none can escape!

3. Benefits Derived from the Exile

The long, hard years of humiliation and sorrow in exile had some distinctly beneficial results in the life of the Jews: (1) They were thoroughly cured of idolatry. Never since then have Jews been idolators. (2) The synagogue came into existence. Back in Jerusalem they had their Temple. This was not available in Babylon so they built smaller houses which served, not only as centers of worship, but also as places for instruction in their law. (3) Religion for them became distinctly more spiritual and personal. The doctrine of individual responsibility was so emphasized by Jeremiah and Ezekiel that the faith of their people came to have much more of the personal element in it. (4) They became a people genuinely united in ideals and purpose. Factional strifes and jealousies practically disappeared and they attained a unity which was highly desirable. They were a "separate" people who were able to stand together against outside influences. (5) They came into a new understanding of their destiny as a nation. They came to be a people with a mission.

II. THE RESTORATION (2 Chron. 36:22–23; Ezra; Neh.; Hag.; Mal.)

The political situation which made it possible for the Jews to return to their native land was the rise of Cyrus of Persia.

Within the space of twenty years he had made himself the ruler of the vast territory from Persia to the continent of Europe. In 539 B.C. Babylon fell to Cyrus. In this way he came to rule over the Jews then in exile.

1. The Decree of Cyrus (2 Chron. 36:22-23; Ezra 1)

In 538 B.C. Cyrus issued his famous decree permitting and encouraging all peoples in exile in his domain to return to their respective homelands. Thus the Jews were allowed to go back home.

We have no way of knowing how many Jews were in Babylonia at the time. It is probably safe to assume that the number was considerably larger than the number taken there from Judah. Whatever may have been the total, it is clear that no large number manifested any great desire to return to the old homeland. According to the Biblical accounts, there were altogether about sixty thousand to return. The first group was led by Zerubbabel, and some time later other groups went back under Ezra and under Nehemiah. We may not be far wrong in assuming that these last two groups were not far apart.

2. Zerubbabel and His Company (Ezra 2-6)

Zerubbabel, a prince of the house of David, was the leader of the group which left in 537 B.C. to return to Jerusalem. To bring this immense company of some fifty thousand people, with their possessions, the long journey of eight hundred miles was a big undertaking. It is said that they received voluntary assistance from friends and also that Cyrus made grants to them. Even with assistance all along the way, it would require faith and real courage to undertake this venture.

The motive for this great undertaking under Zerubbabel was primarily a religious one. They wanted to restore the ancient Temple in Jerusalem. With all the difficulties they encountered, it was twenty years before they had finished rebuilding the Temple. This new building was very modest and humble compared to the glorious structure of Solomon, but it served its purpose and was dedicated in 516 B.C.

3. *Ezra Returns to Jerusalem* (Ezra 7–10; Neh. 8)

Sometime later Ezra, a priest and a scribe, took another group back to Jerusalem. His chief purpose was to lead in the ministry of teaching the law of Moses and in re-establishing the worship of Jehovah. It was in connection with Ezra's work that the synagogue came into existence.

4. *The Contribution of Nehemiah* (Neh.)

The third group of exiles to return from Babylonia to the old homeland was under the general direction of a layman known as Nehemiah. He apparently came from a well-to-do family of Jews living in Susa or Shushan. He rose to the high position of cupbearer of Artaxerxes, king of Persia.

Nehemiah learned of the distressing need of the people back in Jerusalem. The city without walls was defenseless and the people discouraged. The king graciously expressed his sympathetic interest by giving Nehemiah leave of absence to go to Jerusalem and, in addition, provided passport and letters to the officials in Palestine. The king also provided Nehemiah with a royal escort and with authority to secure materials for rebuilding the walls of Jerusalem.

Upon reaching the city, Nehemiah found it in even worse condition than he had anticipated. Acting as governor of the city, he organized the people for the gigantic undertaking of rebuilding the walls. Specific sections were assigned to different groups of workmen, each group under a supervisor. Nehemiah himself remained constantly on the job to push the project. By almost superhuman efforts against desperate opposition, the walls were repaired in the remarkably short space of fifty-two days.

In addition to his work in rebuilding the walls of Jerusalem, Nehemiah rendered great service in reforming the social and religious life of the people. His unselfish and generous nature is shown by the fact that he gave all these years of devoted service to his people without any monetary compensation whatsoever. Without his magnificent contribution, one wonders if this discouraged and struggling little colony could have survived. Nehemiah deserves a place among the greatest benefactors of his race.

We now come to the close of the Old Testament record. The majority of scholars place the time at about 400 B.C., although there is wide difference of opinion on this date. The Jews are at home in Jerusalem, though they are still the subjects of the king of Persia. They are a small group with but few resources. But they are not to be extinguished. Their glorious spiritual mission is yet to be realized.

III. The Interbiblical Period

As we have already noted, the Old Testament closed with the work of Malachi, which many scholars place at about 400 B.C., while others believe the date was much later. The New Testament opens with the birth of Christ.

1. A Period of Significant Changes

The time between the Old Testament and the New is known as the interbiblical period. While the biblical record does not deal with the events of this period, they are important to an understanding of the New Testament. We are, therefore, giving a brief summary of the chief developments during these years. The information on this period is taken from three sources: secular history, the writings of Josephus, and the Apocryphal books.

This history from the restoration period until the New Testament period is made up of four distinct divisions, which we shall consider in proper order in this chapter. These divisions are (1) Persian, 538–332 B.C.; (2) Greek, 332–167 B.C.; (3) Hebrew independence, 167–63 B.C.; (4) Roman, 63 B.C. to A.D. 70.

2. The Jews Under Persian Rule

In the preceding pages we have dealt with the story of Persia's gaining control over the Jews by their conquest of

Babylon in 538 B.C., at which time the Jews became the subjects of Cyrus the Great. So far as the record reveals, the Jews were treated fairly by the Persian rulers, both in Persian territory and in Palestine. Naturally they were not free, but as long as they recognized the supremacy of Persia and observed the law governing them, they were not molested or abused.

When the Old Testament closed, possibly about 400 B.C., the Jewish people in Judah were still the subjects of Persia. This relationship continued, apparently without any outspoken resentment on the part of the Jews, until the Perisan power began to wane and finally came to an end with the swift conquests of Alexander the Great of Greece.

3. *The Conquest of the Greeks*

While Persia continued her domination of southwest Asia, a new power was rising in Europe. This was the little country of Greece. The Persians had crossed the Aegean Sea and had gained a foothold in Greece. Alexander the Great now came to the forefront as the opponent of Persia. He drove the Persians out of Greece, crossed into Asia, and, in the most phenomenal conquest of ancient history, continued his march eastward until he reached ancient India. Naturally Palestine came under his control, and thus the Jews were the subjects of another foreign power.

Alexander treated the Jews generously. At his death his vast empire was divided into four regions. The Jews were wedged between two of these, the Ptolemies in Egypt (323–198 B.C.) and the Seleucids in Syria. Under the Seleucids (198–167 B.C.) the Jews suffered the greatest persecution and indignities in all their history. Finally, in desperation they revolted and organized their limited forces to fight for their freedom.

In a series of brilliant military feats, Judas Maccabeus, the Jewish military leader, defeated the Syrians in four campaigns. These achievements were little less than miraculous. They established Judas Maccabeus as one of the greatest military heroes in Jewish history. The result was the inauguration of an era of Jewish independence which lasted about a century (167–63 B.C.). The Temple was renovated and worship was re-established.

In order to appreciate these achievements one should understand the issues involved. With the conquest by the Greeks, the Jews were brought into contact with western (Greek) civilization for the first time. Hellenism, or the Greek way of life, was radically different from that of the Jews or any other Oriental people.

To the Greek life was good and should be enjoyed. Health was at the foundation. The gymnasium was a popular institution where the young men met for physical exercises and social activities. Activities of all kinds—games, contests, sports, dancing, music, poetry—were emphasized.

Literature and art occupied a prominent place in their lives. Being intellectually alert, they had their schools, their philosophical discussions, their training centers for students of art and sculpture. They developed the most beautiful language of any people in history. It was an instrument of such beauty, precision, and refinement that any other language seemed barbarous in comparison with it. No wonder that the Greek language conquered the world in a short time after the conquests of Alexander.

Greek manners and customs of living also were vastly different from those of Orientals. Their dress was gay, even gaudy, with mantles and broad-brimmed hats. Their emphasis on proper styles and the attention they gave to proper personal appearance would impress the Jews as frivolous, vain, useless, and even wicked.

To the Greeks pleasure of all kinds was not only legitimate but desirable. They believed that life should be enjoyed today—tomorrow we may not have. No wonder Epicureanism became the accepted standard of thought and behavior for most of the Greek people. Religion, particularly as it related to future life, had but little place in their thoughts.

The problem facing the Jews under Greek control was: Could they accept Hellenism and remain loyal to the faith of their fathers? Some felt that they could, and hence a few openly accepted it. The big majority, however, felt that they could not become Hellenists without betraying their faith and that this heathenism must be resisted even unto death.

After the death of Alexander the Great, the Jews were under the control of the Ptolemies (rulers in Egypt) for 125 years (323–198 B.C.). While the Ptolemies were sympathetic to Greek culture, they did not force it upon the Jews. When the Ptolemies were defeated by the Seleucids in 198 B.C., the latter became the rulers of the Jews. Immediately they began a systematic program of compelling the Jews to accept Hellenism. Under Antiochus Epiphanes, the most fanatical Seleucid ruler, the Jews suffered severely. This period of terrible persecution precipitated the new era of Hebrew independence.

4. Hebrew Independence

Sometimes the darkest hour is just before dawn. It proved to be so at this time. When the situation looked altogether hopeless for the Hebrew people, an event took place which changed their history. An aged priest named Mattathias, goaded to despair by the Seleucids, slew the emissary of the king and then made a passionate appeal to the Jewish people to rise up and resist their rulers. A miracle occurred when unexpectedly thousands of Jews rallied to the cause ready to die for their faith. This new army was headed by Judas Maccabeus, the son of Mattathias. In four successive encounters, Judas defeated the enemy's much larger armies. A new surge of enthusiasm and patriotism resulted in the freedom of the Jews, and in the establishment of their independence—their first freedom since the Babylonian exile.

The period of Hebrew independence started auspiciously. At first their leaders were devout worshipers of Jehovah. As time passed, the glamor and fervor passed, and baser ideals prevailed. Near the end of this period the Jews were hopelessly involved in internal strife and rivalry, which made them an easy victim for the new world power which was to envelop them.

5. *The Conquest by the Romans*

Back west, in the center of the Mediterranean world, Rome had been growing and expanding. Already the armies of Rome had made significant conquests in Europe and North Africa. They now moved toward the east, conquered Greece, and then crossed into Asia Minor. So, in 63 B.C., Pompey, the Roman general, was in Syria looking down into Palestine. The rival parties of the Jews both hurried to Pompey for assistance. The haughty Roman had only to speak the word in order to conquer the Jews. In 63 B.C. Rome conquered Palestine and made it a province of the vast Roman Empire, which covered the Mediterranean world.

Sixty years before Jesus was born, his people became the subjects of Rome. They continued to live in their ancestral land, but they were surrounded by Greek culture and were dominated by the powerful Roman rulers. Thus Christ was born and lived all his earthly life under Roman rule. While, to the Jewish people, the status of an occupied country was an unhappy existence, at the same time it had its advantages. The Roman Empire provided just the situation needed to make Christianity the religion of the Gentiles and to give it the necessary start in its program of conquest of the world.

6. *Preparation for the Advent of Jesus Christ*

While not all the events included in this period are to be found in the Bible, it is easy to see the hand of God in these experiences of his people. As the Jews entered upon the hard and bitter times in exile, they seem to have made adjustments and, through the ministry of several prophets, came to a fuller understanding of God's purposes for them.

Looking back over the years when they were the subjects of Persia, Greece, and Rome, we can see how God was preparing the Jews and the world for the advent of Jesus Christ. Greek culture and learning contributed to this preparation. The strong Roman government provided a happy situation for the spread of the gospel after the death and resurrection of Jesus. The Jews were scattered over all the Mediterranean world; Greek was the spoken language of all these nations; and Rome had created an era free from war. The situation was just right for the coming of Jesus Christ. As Paul stated, "When the fulness of the time was come, God sent forth his Son" (Gal. 4:4).

FOR CLASS DISCUSSION AND FURTHER STUDY

1. On a map mark the lands to which Israel and Judah were taken in their captivity.
2. As you continue tracing the unfolding story of God's plan of redemption, do you consider that God's purpose in the Babylonian exile was primarily to punish his people or to purify and discipline them? What contributions did their experiences during the exile make toward their development culturally, religiously, and politically?
3. How did the period "between the Testaments" help to prepare for the earthly ministry of Jesus and the spread of Christianity?

CHAPTER 7

I. POETRY IN THE OLD TESTAMENT
1. The Book of Job
2. The Psalms
3. The Proverbs
4. Ecclesiastes
5. The Song of Solomon
6. Lamentations

II. THE PROPHETS OF ISRAEL
1. The Work of a Prophet
2. The List of Prophets
3. Some Early Prophets
4. Prophets During the Assyrian Crisis (Eighth Century)
5. Prophets During the Chaldean Crisis (Seventh Century)
6. Prophets During the Exile (Sixth Century)
7. Later Prophets

III. CONCLUSION

7

The Poets and the Prophets of Israel

THUS FAR, in our study of the Old Testament we have given major emphasis to the historical record. While this history is basic, we should not overlook the important contribution made by the teachers in the Old Testament. We are, therefore, devoting one chapter to the poets and the prophets of the Hebrew people.

I. POETRY IN THE OLD TESTAMENT

The poems of the Old Testament, particularly the Psalms and Proverbs, are known and loved by millions of readers. No other poems are so cherished and so continuously studied and appreciated as the works of the singers of Israel. Many scholars hold that the poetry of the Old Testament is the most significant contribution of the Hebrew people to the literature of the world.

There are six books in the Old Testament usually classified as poetry: Job, Psalms, Proverbs, Ecclesiastes, Song of Solomon, and Lamentations. However, Hebrew poetry is not confined to these books. The student using an American Standard Version or any later translation of the Bible will easily discover many brief poems outside these books. These poems are found in the earliest books such as Genesis 4:19–23; Numbers 21:14–15; Judges 5, and so on. Again, special occasions, such as marriages and victory in war, usually were celebrated with song and dance. The golden age of Hebrew poetry was during the reigns of David and Solomon, though many Old Testament poems belong both before and after this period.

Poetry of the Old Testament is quite different from ordinary poetry, in that it has neither rhyme nor meter. Hebrew poetry resembles our free verse and consequently suffers but little in translation. Generally speaking the poems of the Old Testament may be classified as follows: (1) lyric, the poetry of sentiment; (2) dramatic as in Job; (3) proverbial; and (4) elegiac.

1. *The Book of Job*

Job is one of the most remarkable books ever written. It is dramatic poetry, conversation, and argument, in dignified and exalted language. The fact that we know neither the date nor the author of this book does not minimize its significance. There are three well defined divisions of the book: (1) the prologue (chaps. 1–2) in prose; (2) the main body or the arguments (chaps. 3–41) in exalted poetry; and (3) the epilogue (chap. 42) in prose. The book deals with one of the profoundest and most puzzling problems of human life: Why do the righteous suffer? The purpose of this book seems to be to disprove the theory that suffering or misfortune is a sign of divine displeasure and is always brought upon men by their own sins.

2. *The Psalms*

The most familiar part of the Old Testament is the book of Psalms, or parts of it. The average reader, who may not have the time nor the inclination to study the books of history or law or prophecy, will find himself reading the book of Psalms frequently. This is true partly because these are poems which can be read quickly and easily. Perhaps the real reason is that he finds in these great devotional poems the thing which he needs.

The book is a collection of poems covering a long period in the history of Israel. They were composed and used for a wide variety of occasions or purposes. Many of them are hymns which were used in worship. No doubt many of these were set to music and were used in the liturgy of Temple worship, though naturally the music has not been preserved. Since these poems cover a period of a thousand years or more, they were written by many different people. It is customary to think of David as the author of many of these. Scholars are agreed that some seventy-five were written by this poet king.

The psalms express every emotion of the human heart. Martin Luther called the book of Psalms a "Bible in miniature." Many of these familiar poems deal with the meaning of life and death. A large number of them furnish the finest expression of personal faith in God. The book of Psalms has done more to mold the language and form of public worship and private devotions than any other book. In Old Testament times, these songs were the models of worship, of prayer and adoration, of penitence and hope, of praise and thanksgiving. Even to the present time no one has improved on them.

3. The Proverbs

A proverb is a short, pithy, axiomatic saying. Lord John Russell defined a proverb as a maxim which contains "the wisdom of many and the wit of one." This type of literature was especially beloved by Oriental people, including the Hebrews. The book of Proverbs is a collection of wise sayings written over a period of hundreds of years. No doubt Solomon wrote many of these, but certainly not all of them. The book is not theoretical or speculative, but is exceedingly practical in nature. It is concerned with conduct, behavior or wise living. It has been called "A Business Manual for Young Men" since its constant appeal is to young men. The object seems to be to inspire young men to honesty, purity, and industry.

4. Ecclesiastes

We may consider Ecclesiastes as a book of poetry, though some scholars would not agree. The Hebrew word translated "ecclesiastes" means preacher or proclaimer, and signifies one who calls together and addresses an audience. The book represents the experience of a man who had the best of everything—wealth, rank, honor, fame, and pleasure—and who, at the end, was disillusioned. He felt the emptiness of all such so-called blessings and concluded that all was "vanity and vexation of spirit." The word vanity is used about thirty times in the book of Ecclesiastes.

The purpose of the book seems to be to show that self-gratification and successful worldliness do not bring satisfaction to the human heart. Life without a knowledge of and fellowship with God is empty and meaningless. Man has a destiny which calls for co-operation with God in some worthy enterprise, and in this he finds abiding peace of soul. The book ends with the familiar injunction: "Fear God, and keep his commandments: for this is the whole duty of man" (Eccl. 12:13).

5. *The Song of Solomon*

The Song of Solomon, sometimes called the Song of Songs or Canticles, is one of the strangest books in the Old Testament. It is a love song, or perhaps a collection of love songs, which were greatly admired by Oriental peoples. It abounds in metaphors and enters freely into the description of physical beauty and charm. There are some who hold that the Song of Solomon is allegorical, portraying the relation between Christ and the church. Many scholars hold that this poem was written to celebrate the strength, the beauty, and the constancy of human love. These contend that the importance of a strong, clean love between man and woman, on which the home is built, is sufficient justification for placing this book in the list of inspired writings in the Bible.

6. *Lamentations*

The book of Lamentations is an elegy or funeral dirge over the desolation of Jerusalem after its destruction by Nebuchadnezzar. It was written by Jeremiah, and was at one time a part of the book which bears his name. The book describes vividly the wretched condition of the wasted city, together with the horrors of its siege. The inspired writer holds that the cause of the desolation of the people was their sins against Jehovah.

II. THE PROPHETS OF ISRAEL

The most powerful and influential teachers in the Old Testament were the prophets. Teaching was their chief function; for this they were called and commissioned. They stood as the direct spokesmen of God. They received their messages from God and gave them directly to the people as the truth revealed by God. They served in times of crisis and helped determine the cause of Hebrew history.

1. *The Work of a Prophet*

In the Hebrew language the chief words used to describe the prophet are *Ro'eh* and *Chozeh,* which mean to see, and *Nabhi,* which means to announce or proclaim. Hence the prophet was one who had received a message from God and who delivered it as the word of God.

The work of the prophets extends over a period of several hundred years, certainly from the time of the judges to the close of the Old Testament. The period of greatest prophetic activity was during the time of the kingdom, especially during the latter years of both Israel and Judah.

There were many prophets whose messages have not been preserved in book form. These men exerted a great influence but did not write books. Elijah and Elisha are good examples of this type. Others have left their books to be included in our Bible. There are sixteen books of prophecy in the Old Testament. (Jeremiah and Lamentations were originally one book.) These are called major prophets (four books) and minor prophets (twelve books). It should be pointed out that the terms "major" and "minor" do not refer to the relative importance of their work, but rather to the length or the brevity of their books.

Usually the prophets were men called forth by a crisis or an emergency, to declare the will of the Lord. They were prominent in the field of statesmanship. They were well informed students of the affairs of their day, both national and international. They gave advice to the kings and statesmen of the day with all confidence and with the expectation that their message would be heeded as the word of Jehovah. The priest was to perform the routine duties in the services of the sanctuary. The prophet was the independent and authoritative voice to speak forth the message for the time.

2. The List of Prophets

While there is some difference of opinion among scholars on the exact date when these men worked, and consequently of the precise order in which they came, the grouping and the dates given seem to be reasonably accurate.

Naturally a full appreciation of the work of each prophet depends upon an intelligent understanding of the circumstances in which he worked. Nevertheless it is true that their messages are independent of time and have a distinct value for every age.

3. Some Early Prophets

The earliest of the Old Testament prophets were Moses (about 1450 B.C.), Samuel (1100 B.C.), Elijah (870 B.C.), Elisha (850 B.C.), Joel (840 B.C.), and Jonah (800 B.C.).

Of the six prophets listed we will consider only two, Joel and Jonah, since the works of the other four have been studied in connection with the historical record of their respective periods.

(1) *Joel* (840 B.C.).—Joel is a very brief book having only three chapters. The prophet's message was called forth by a national calamity. There had been a devastating plague of locusts which had left the land stripped of food. This was followed by a famine, with resulting poverty and misery. These calamities created a situation that called for the sure word of Jehovah. Joel came forth to speak for God in this dark hour. It is probable that he spoke far more than is included in his book. The book itself has two distinct divisions. The first (1:1 to 2:27) is a call to repentance and prayer. In the second (2:28 to 3:21) Jehovah promises to hear the cry of his people, to remove the cause of their sufferings and to restore prosperity and enrich them spiritually.

(2) *Jonah* (800 B.C.).—The story of Jonah is one of great

significance and value. He lived in the time just preceding the Assyrian invasion and the downfall of Israel in 722 B.C. The account of his attempt to escape the call of God to go to Ninevah, his final acceptance of this call, and the result of his preaching in Ninevah points up the unmistakable message of the book, the concern of Jehovah for all peoples, regardless of race or nationality. We have here the message of "foreign missions" eight hundred years before the birth of Christ.

4. *Prophets During the Assyrian Crisis* (Eighth Century)

The period preceding the Assyrian captivity was marked by persistent moral decline in the Northern Kingdom. In both Israel and Judah God used prophets to warn the people of judgment.

(1) *Amos* (760 B.C.).—This prophet of righteousness lived in the reign of Jeroboam II of Israel. The student will recall that this was an era of great national expansion accompanied by almost unparalleled national prosperity. Assyria, which had been spared because of the preaching of Jonah, was now rising up, preparing to reach toward the Mediterranean in a program of conquest.

Amos came forth with his message to save his people from disaster. In his condemnation of their wickedness he mentions almost every sin conceivable—immorality, drunkenness, theft, greed, injustice, disregard of the poor, defrauding the helpless, neglect of spiritual duties, and forsaking of Jehovah their God. Outwardly the people were religious, taking pains to attend the proper ceremonies, observe the technical regulations, and make the required offerings. Inwardly, however, they were selfish, cruel, wicked, and worldly-minded.

The book gives an authentic picture of internal conditions in Israel in one of its most important periods. It has value as an illustration of the message of a great prophet and the manner in which he worked. Its practical value to us lies in its truths which relate to our own day. The key statement of Amos' message may be found in 5:24 "Let justice roll down as waters, and righteousness as a mighty stream" (ASV).

(2) *Hosea* (750 B.C.).—The prophet Hosea may be considered a contemporary of Amos, though he probably did his work some ten years later. Apparently the faithful ministry of Amos had not produced any permanent reformation. The same sins still blighted the land and Israel still seemed unaware of danger and unresponsive to the gracious mercies and proffered guidance of Jehovah their God.

We know but little of the background of Hosea. He was a native of the Northern Kingdom and in this kingdom he did all his work as a prophet. The bitter tragedy of his marriage did something for Hosea that nothing but suffering and sorrow can do. He was forced to drink deeply of the cup of woe as well as of the spring of joy. This experience enabled him to understand something of God's immeasurable love for his people. It enabled him also to plead with his people effectively to return to their God who loved them. The entire experience came to be a sort of living analogy of God's relation to Israel. Thus the message of Hosea is one of the tenderest and most appealing of all the prophets. For pathos and beauty it is unsurpassed. Amos preached to the conscience; Hosea appealed to the heart. Both were prophets of real repentance.

(3) *Isaiah* (740–698 B.C.).—Isaiah belongs at the head of all lists of the prophets. In him prophecy reaches perhaps its highest standards. As one enthusiastic critic has put it, Isaiah has all the great qualities of all the prophets. In the length of his service, in the critical issues he faced, in the content of his message, in the effectiveness of his work and in the quality of his written messages, he excels them all.

He was of an aristocratic family, the son of Amoz, who is said to have been the brother of king Amaziah. He received his call (Isa. 6) in the year that Uzziah died, and for some fifty years lived and served in Jerusalem. He was married and had two sons.

The prophet lived in the critical days of the Assyrian domination. Within the first twenty-five years of his ministry the Assyrians captured Samaria and ended the Northern Kingdom (722 B.C.). Twenty-one years later the same pagan foes stood at the gates of Jerusalem and would have captured the Southern Kingdom also but for the miraculous intervention of Jehovah through Isaiah, his messenger (Isa. 36:1 to 37:37).

The greatest problems faced by Judah were not military. This Assyrian invasion raised many racial and religious problems which called for the courage and wisdom of the great Isaiah. He stood firm against idolatry and every other sin which threatened to overwhelm the little kingdom of Judah during these critical years. This brilliant, cultured, and consecrated servant of God, the trusted counselor of kings, worked for fifty years at the very heart of the life of the nation.

The book of Isaiah is the noblest in prophetic literature, if not in all the Old Testament. It is most like the New Testament and is far more frequently quoted in the New Testament than any other. The reader who spends most of his time in the New Testament will be surprised to discover how much of its meaning and even its language is taken from Isaiah. The book is a long one of sixty-six chapters.

(4) *Micah* (735 B.C.).—A contemporary of Isaiah, Micah lived under the same conditions and faced the same problems. Isaiah did his work in the city, while Micah seems to have worked with people out in the country. He came from the little village of Moresheth on the borders between Judah and Philistia, a distance of about twenty-five miles southwest of Jerusalem. His home was on the main highway between Jerusalem and Egypt, and because of this the young prophet had opportunities to learn of big events taking place in his time. We know almost nothing of his family or of his home life. His work indicates that in some way he had an unusual knowledge of social abuses and civic corruption. He had a vital knowledge of the elements of real religion, and he had courage to declare the truth as he understood it. He championed the cause of the poor against the oppressions of the rich. He loved all his country but was especially devoted to his own poor and oppressed people. He preached righteousness and justice with flaming words. His words were effec-

tive because the reasons for his passionate proclamations were so evident: "Pinched peasant faces peer between all his words."

5. *Prophets During the Chaldean Crisis* (Seventh Century)

After the Northern Kingdom was overthrown and its people taken into captivity by the Assyrians, God continued to send his warnings to the Southern Kingdom through his prophets.

(1) *Zephaniah* (625 B.C.).—This prophet was of aristocratic lineage. Some scholars hold that he was related to Josiah, who at the time was king of Judah. If so, this background enabled him to speak effectively on the sins of his time.

It will be recalled that the chief event in the reign of Josiah, king of Judah, was his reformation. This was a nationwide movement backed by the deepest conviction of the young king. It is likely that Zephaniah supported the reforms of Josiah. The young prophet had accurate knowledge of conditions in the city of Jerusalem where he probably lived all his life. He took a dark view of the situation and offered only one hope, namely, turning to Jehovah, the God of Israel.

(2) *Jeremiah* (625–585 B.C.).—The prophet Jeremiah, had a ministry of some forty years during the last years of the kingdom of Judah and the early part of the Babylonian captivity. It was his hard lot to witness the death of a nation and the discouraging prospect of exile in a foreign land. In later years Jeremiah had to kindle the hopes of the people and undergird their faith when they faced the certainty of exile. He did not go with the exiles to Babylon, though he wrote them and sought to encourage them in the hope of mercy in the future.

Jeremiah was, by all means, the chief figure of his time, towering above every man in the period. He was a patriot, a prophet and statesman, a wise counselor of kings, and a courageous foe of wickedness and sin. By nature he was sensitive, timid, and melancholy. He had no home, no family, and much of the time no friends. His life was practically that of a martyr, but he bore his sufferings without complaint or bitterness.

Jeremiah made two distinctive contributions to the revelation of religious truth: (1) True religion is essentially spiritual in nature. (2) Personal responsibility is inescapable. These concepts constituted a mighty step forward.

(3) *Nahum* (625 B.C.).—The prophet Nahum belonged to the same period as Jeremiah. His hatred for the cruel Assyrians can be detected in almost every sentence of his book. The theme of the book is that a holy and just God could not let the wicked city of Nineveh live. Nahum's righteous indignation flashes like lightning in poetic utterance, yet he shows that God's wrath and vengeance are not to be thought of as the petty blunderings of men. "God is the master of his wrath and uses it." When God is angry it is because of principle and not caprice. This city, guilty of cruelty, harlotry, brutality, oppression, and rebellion against God, must reap the awful consequences. Nineveh had mocked God and must die. Such teaching is not inconsistent with the holiness of God.

(4) *Habakkuk* (610 B.C.).—We know but little about the man Habakkuk except by inference from his book. He probably was an eye witness to the first ravages of Jerusalem by the armies of Nebuchadnezzar. His spirit was deeply troubled by these momentous events. How could a righteous God permit so much suffering and death? He was an honest seeker of the truth who went directly to God for the answer. In a "watchtower" experience the prophet learned that God was working through the adversities to lead his people to repentance. The hand of God was moving purposefully and lovingly.

6. *Prophets During the Exile* (Sixth Century)

Even though the kingdom of Judah suffered God's judgment, she was not abandoned by the Almighty. He continued to send his word to his people through prophets.

(1) *Daniel* (590 B.C.).—Probably born in Jerusalem, Dan-

iel was among those Jews first taken into Babylonian captivity (606 B.C.). He was selected for special service by
Nebuchadnezzar and served with distinction in the government. In all his experiences he never compromised his con-
victions nor wavered in his loyalty to Jehovah his God. He
lived through the entire period of the exile and probably
died in Babylon. By his example and teaching he was a
mighty influence among the Jews. He believed and taught
that God would deliver his servants. He was confident of
the final triumph of the kingdom of God.

His book is apocalyptic in nature, containing visions that
are variously interpreted. However, there is much in it that
can be understood by all who studiously read it. The book
contains two very obvious sections: Daniel's personal experiences (chaps. 1–6) and his visions of the kingdom
(chaps. 7–12).

(2) *Ezekiel* (590 B.C.).—In the second group of exiles,
taken to Babylon in 597 B.C., was Ezekiel, who had been a
priest in Jerusalem. He was probably well acquainted with
Daniel. Ezekiel's work differed somewhat from that of most
of the other prophets. He did not so much predict or forecast
events as to record visions of these. In his book there are
many symbols, visions, parables, and allegories, some of
which are concerned with future events and some with exist-
ing facts and conditions. His book, when properly understood, is a significant literary and religious volume containing
addresses and appeals which are very practical.

Ezekiel's mission was chiefly to destroy the false hopes
held by so many exiles of an early return to Jerusalem. God
had a purpose in the exile; they were to remain in Babylonia
a long time to learn this lesson. They must rethink their faith
and learn the larger spiritual mission of their race. Ezekiel
was to serve as their spiritual guide, to warn against apostasy,
to console, to stimulate, and to enhearten them. For twenty-
two years he worked at his discouraging and difficult task.
The people of Israel and the entire world are more deeply
indebted to this faithful and unselfish "watchman" and interpreter than we will ever know. Without him the faith of

God's people might not have survived the hard years of captivity.

(3) *Obadiah* (585 B.C.).—The book of Obadiah, with its one chapter of twenty-one verses, is the shortest book in the Old Testament. Its author lived at the same time as Ezekiel and Jeremiah. He was deeply offended by the lack of sympathy and even the delight which the Edomites exhibited in the destruction of Jerusalem by the Babylonians. His book is an oration directed against Edom for this unbrotherly behavior and a message of hope for the faithful in Israel.

7. *Later Prophets*

Three of the prophetic books of the Old Testament are by prophets who ministered during the restoration period.

(1) *Haggai* (520 B.C.).—This prophet belongs to the latter part of the exile in Babylon. He was born in Babylon and was in the company of Zerubbabel, which returned to Jerusalem under the decree of Cyrus to rebuild the Temple. Haggai began his ministry during the rebuilding and was the first prophet in Jerusalem after the return. His chief objective was to stimulate and encourage the Jews in their big undertaking of reconstructing the Temple and of reinstituting their worship.

(2) *Zechariah* (520 B.C.).—Zechariah was contemporary with Haggai, hence the background of his work is the same. He stood with the older prophet and gave his strength and energies to the same great objective. He has been called the prophet with "the soul of an artist and the eye of a seer."

(3) *Malachi* (435 B.C.).—The last of the prophets, Malachi lived and labored in the restored community of Jerusalem. Many changes had occurred since the times of Haggai and Zechariah. The people had grown indifferent to their spiritual obligations and had neglected the Temple. They were worldly, restless, and in danger from their enemies about them. The prophet insisted that God's acceptance of men's offerings and service is conditioned upon the sincerity and purity of the life of those who make them. The people had robbed God, not only in tithes and offerings, but in with-

holding from him their loyalty and their love. Malachi proclaimed that, if the people would give to God what rightfully belonged to him, abundant blessings should follow.

III. CONCLUSION

In closing this chapter we may point out one fact of great significance. The truth of God is both timeless and timely. The spiritual content of Job, Psalms, Proverbs, and other books of poetry is applicable to our day. Likewise the messages of the great prophets of Israel will always be appropriate. The sins they denounced are evident in the life of every generation. The admonitions they gave are appropriate for today. The principles they proclaimed so vigorously are needed in modern life. Each prophet was called forth for a particular situation. His message was for that situation, but not for it alone. He uttered truths which will continue to meet the needs of every generation.

FOR CLASS DISCUSSION AND FURTHER STUDY

1. Refer to the chart suggested as further study for chapter 5. As you consider each prophet discussed in chapter 7, recall what you have learned about the king, or kings, who ruled during the time the prophet ministered. Try to decide how the prophet's message was particularly suited to the conditions which existed in his day.
2. As you consider the main theme of each prophet's message, discuss its pertinence for our own time.
3. Discuss ways in which the writings of the Old Testament poets and prophets helped to pass on the story of redemption. As you read the books of Old Testament poetry and prophecy, look for statements about God's plan for saving man through a coming Redeemer.

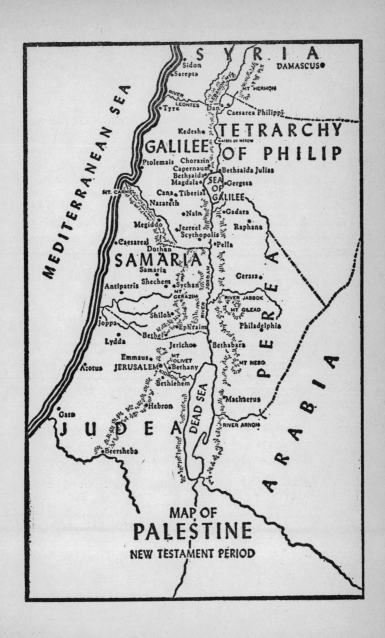

MAP OF
PALESTINE
NEW TESTAMENT PERIOD

CHAPTER 8

8

The Earthly Life of Jesus Christ

THE MOST AMAZING movement in all history is the one which arose with Jesus Christ and his disciples. This movement was launched by Jesus during the "days of his flesh" in Palestine more than nineteen hundred years ago and has been carried on by his disciples since his death. The most meaningful book in all literature is the New Testament, our only authentic record of this historic enterprise.

By any and all standards Jesus Christ is universally regarded as the greatest figure in human history. During his earthly lifetime no one understood or even dreamed of the influence which the work of Jesus would have on the history of the world. It is possible now, however, for the student of history to look back upon these two thousand years and understand to some degree the revolutionary, beneficent, and far-reaching influence which the teachings of Jesus, together with his death and resurrection, have had upon the races of mankind.

I. THE WORLD INTO WHICH JESUS WAS BORN

Jesus lived in the Roman world of the first Christian century. His home was in Palestine, a tiny province of the vast Roman empire that completely surrounded the Mediterranean Sea. The civilization of this century was dominated by the language and philosophy of Greece, together with the practical and efficient organization of the Roman government. The Jews struggled desperately to maintain their loyalty to the teachings of their fathers but they were naturally affected by these Greco-Roman influences. Roman soldiers stationed in Palestine enforced the laws, supported by Roman courts.

Palestine, the homeland of Jesus, was divided into six political regions. West of the Jordan River, to the south was Judah; north of Judah was Samaria; while north of this was the hill country of Galilee, the home of Jesus. East of the Jordan were the provinces of Perea, the Decapolis, and the mountainous area north of the Sea of Galilee.

Economic life was quite simple. There were no industries and no important trading activities. The people were very poor and lived simply in their humble homes. The chief political figure in Palestine was Herod the Great, who died during the early childhood of Jesus (Matt. 2:19). After his death, the country was ruled by procurators.

The religious life of the Jews centered in the Temple at Jerusalem and in the many local synagogues where their religion was taught. The two big religious parties were the Pharisees (conservatives) and the Sadducees (liberals). The ecclesiastical court whose function was to decide questions of a religious nature was the Sanhedrin, made up of about seventy members. The chief characteristic of Jewish religious life was the strict adherence to the traditions of their fathers, which had deteriorated into cold, lifeless ritual.

II. THE BIRTH AND BOYHOOD OF JESUS (Matt. 1-2; Luke 1-2)

To reduce the record of the earthly life of Jesus into a few pages is an almost impossible task. However, we can seek to put the most significant events in proper chronological order, without any effort to interpret them.

At the outset we may state that there are miracles in the life of Jesus. The New Testament opens with supernatural events and the Gospels close with the record of the resurrection and ascension of Jesus. The existence of Jesus goes back to the beginning of time. He existed as the Son of God long before he was born as a child in Bethlehem. The great miracle in the birth of Jesus is the incarnation, that is, God becoming human flesh. Jesus lived in the flesh some thirty-three years and then went "back to the Father."

Since the four Gospels do not present the details in the life of Jesus in chronological order, we have no way of marking the exact time and place of all these events. The general order, however, is clear; and we need not to be overly concerned about chronology.

All the facts about the birth of Jesus are given by Matthew and Luke. The story of his advent begins with the annunciations. The angel Gabriel made three announcements: one to Zacharias the priest, one to Mary in Nazareth, and one to Joseph. These announcements are significant in that they break the long silence of four hundred years and herald the beginning of momentous events.

Zacharias was informed that he was to be the father of John the Baptist. Mary received the news that she was to become the mother of Jesus. Joseph received his visitation to assure him that Mary was not untrue to him: "For that which is conceived in her is of the Holy Spirit" (Matt. 1:20 ASV). Jesus was born of a virgin; he was not the son of Joseph, or of any other man, but the Son of God.

The Roman census issued about this time made it necessary for Joseph to go to his ancestral home in Bethlehem. Mary being "great with child" went with him. There in a stable the boy Jesus was born. The exact time cannot be positively established. It probably occurred in the fall of the year 5 or 4 B.C.

While there in Bethlehem, Jesus was worshiped by the shepherds, was circumcised on the eighth day, and later was presented in the Temple. Some time later the Magi came from the East to worship him. Because of the infamous decree of Herod the Great that the babies of Bethlehem were to be slaughtered, Joseph and Mary took Jesus for a stay in Egypt.

After several months Herod died, and Joseph and Mary then brought Jesus back to Palestine. They were told to take him to Nazareth in Galilee. Here Jesus grew up. Joseph and Mary had four sons (James, Joses, Judah [Juda or Judas], and Simon) and at least two daughters (Mark 6:3). In this humble but happy home Jesus grew to manhood. The only fact recorded of these early years before he began his ministry is his visit to Jerusalem with Joseph and Mary when he

was twelve years old. Here in Nazareth he lived the life of a
normal boy, except without sin.

III. JOHN THE BAPTIST (Luke 1; 3; 7; 9; Matt. 3; 14; John 1; 3)

The son promised to Zacharias and Elizabeth was born as
promised by Gabriel. He was named John and was to be
the forerunner to prepare the way for Jesus. He grew up in
the hill country of Judea and was specially prepared for his
unique ministry.

A new epoch opens with the work of John. He spoke with
the authority of a prophet and his work evoked a response
like that of the prophets of old. It was in A.D. 25 or 26 when
this new prophet, now about thirty years old, broke the
silence and began to stir the hearts of the people. He selected
the valley of the Jordan River as the scene of his labors, and
moved up and down this historic valley with his message.

John could announce the approach of the Messiah, but he
must also declare that the people were not ready for Messiah's coming. The kingdom was to be characterized by
righteousness and holiness, and only those who possessed
these qualities could have any part in it. All others were to
be rejected as the chaff, which the farmer winnows away
with his fan, and as the fruitless tree, which is cut down by
the husbandman. To proclaim such a message required
courage. It called for confession of sin, prayer for forgiveness,
and willingness to be obedient. John's key word was repent.
Again and again he denounced sin in every quarter and
called men to repentance.

Multitudes came to hear this powerful preacher. He por-
trayed the coming Messiah in vivid language. He stirred the
nation with hope and expectation. In one of the companies
who came to hear him was Jesus, who was just six months
younger than John. John baptized him and presented him as
the Messiah. Even after Jesus had entered upon his public
ministry, John continued to preach. In his fearless denunciation of sin he reproved Herod Antipas and Herodias for
their adulterous union. For this he was imprisoned and later
beheaded.

John had done faithfully what he came to do. He aroused the nation; he denounced the sins of the people; he called them to repentance; he announced the kingdom of God; he baptized and presented the Messiah. He was loyal to the last.

IV. THE BEGINNING OF JESUS' MINISTRY (Matt. 3–4; Luke 3–4; John 1–4)

Scholars are not agreed as to the length of Jesus' public ministry, though the majority think of it as about forty months (winter A.D. 26 to spring A.D. 29). It is probable that his baptism took place late in the winter or early in the spring and that his death came at the Passover season three and a fraction years later.

After his baptism by John the Baptist, who publicly presented him, Jesus went up into the high hills of Judea for the temptations, which lasted forty days. He then came down again to the valley where John was preaching. Two disciples of John the Baptist then followed Jesus. These were Andrew and John, who soon enlisted their brothers, Simon Peter and James. These four then went with Jesus up to Galilee. At Cana, Jesus performed his first miracle. After a visit at Capernaum, Jesus then went to Jerusalem, where he had his memorable conference with Nicodemus. After a stay in Jerusalem and a brief trip through Judea, Jesus went back to Galilee, choosing purposely to go through Samaria. Here at Jacob's well he met and won the Samaritan woman and a number of other Samaritans. Back in Galilee he was ready to begin his notable Galilean ministry.

V. THE LONG GALILEAN MINISTRY (Matt. 4–13; Mark 1–6; Luke 4–9)

Jesus began his work in Galilee in the summer or early fall of the year A.D. 26 or 27. The length of this ministry was about eighteen months. During these months, he went to his home city, Nazareth, where he was openly rejected and driven out. He then went to Capernaum on the lake (the Sea of Galilee), which seems to have served as his headquarters, although he made at least three separate tours of the province during these months. This ministry is known as the year of public favor. Jesus' popularity was tremendous.

1. *The Call of the Twelve* (Mark 3 : 13–19; Luke 6 : 12–16)

After a few months, Jesus selected twelve men to be his disciples. From now on they were to be with him constantly for training which would equip them to carry on his work after his death. Having selected these men after a night of prayer, Jesus then gave the famous Sermon on the Mount, which was a sort of inaugural address in which he set forth the principles which must characterize those who are in his kingdom. During these months Jesus gave some of his most famous parables.

2. *The Period of Greatest Popularity*

Two main factors contributed to the growing popularity of Jesus: (1) He performed a great many miracles. These extraordinary works of healing and other miracles were the cause of the widest publicity. (2) His words were heard with wonder and amazement. His enemies themselves bore witness that "never man spake like this man" (John 7:46). A message given by a man of such character would attract and challenge people. A new voice was being heard. The people could not analyze it and did not fully understand it, but they responded to it.

While the Galilean ministry was marked by great public favor, a situation developed which made it necessary for Jesus to adopt a new course in his ministry. The large crowds who followed him came to be more interested in his supplying their need of food and healing their sicknesses than in his spiritual kingdom. They could not understand the true nature of his mission.

VI. THE CLOSING YEAR OF HIS MINISTRY (Matt. 14–20; Mark 6–10; Luke 9–18; John 6–11)

The last year was the hardest. The opposition to Jesus was growing more bitter. It gradually increased during this last year and finally culminated in his death on the cross.

1. Special Training of the Twelve (Mark 6–8; Luke 9; Matt. 14–18; John 6–7)

At the close of the Galilean ministry, Jesus took his disciples away for a period of rest up in the hills to the north. They needed the rest; he needed to give them uninterrupted teaching; and they needed to get away from those opposing his work. This period of special instruction lasted about six months (April–September). During this time there were really four withdrawals which took them into areas north and east of Galilee: (1) beyond the lake (Mark 6:30–44; Luke 9:10–17; Matt. 14:13–21); (2) to the region of Tyre and Sidon (Matt. 7:24–30; Mark 15:21–28); (3) through Phoenicia and around Mount Hermon and Decapolis (Mark 7:31 to 8:9; Matt. 15:29–38); (4) to the region of Bethsaida (Mark 8:13–26; Matt. 16:5–12). The big events in this time were Jesus' special testing of the disciples, which elicited from Peter the famous statement, "Thou art the Christ, the Son of the living God," (Matt. 16:16) and, shortly after this, the transfiguration. Jesus and his disciples came back to Galilee for a brief time and then went to Jerusalem.

2. Later Ministry in Judea (John 7–10; Luke 10–13)

The ministry to Jerusalem was from September to December of Jesus' last year. Again Jerusalem proved to be cold and unresponsive. A visit out in the country of Judea was more encouraging, since the common people believed on Jesus. This period was marked by the bitter controversy with the Jewish leaders in Jerusalem. Jesus sent out seventy disciples into Judea, who came back with enthusiastic reports of their ministry. After the Feast of Dedication in December, Jesus left the city not to return until the last week of his earthly life.

3. The Perean Ministry (John 10–11; Luke 13–19; Matt. 19–20; Mark 10)

From Jerusalem, Jesus went to the Jordan Valley for a brief ministry and then back to Galilee. After a short stay in

Galilee, he began his long and unhurried journey through Perea on his way to Jerusalem for the last week. During this Perean ministry many of the most significant truths were uttered by Jesus. He dealt with the cost of discipleship, the nature and necessity of prayer, the necessity for exercising mercy, and the universal nature of his mission. During this time he visited Bethany where he had previously raised Lazarus from the dead. He came down to the Jordan River, spent a day in Jericho, and then went to Bethany near Jerusalem on Friday, one week before his crucifixion was to take place.

VII. THE LAST WEEK (Matt. 21–27; Mark 11–15; Luke 19–22; John 11–18)

1. *Importance of This Week*

As much as we value the other events in the life of our Lord, we consider the experiences of this week in Jerusalem the most precious heritage of the Christian faith. The four Gospel writers, recognizing the great significance of these last days in the earthly life of Jesus, devote approximately forty per cent of their space to these events.

In the treatment of the events of this week we shall follow the day-by-day order that is accepted by a majority of scholars. However, the New Testament does not state the day for each event, and we cannot be sure of the chronology for the last week. These events occurred during the great Passover feast which came in the spring of the year.

As we move with Jesus from one experience to another in this tragic week we are impressed with his composure, his dignity, and his complete self-possession. The grandeur of his character stands out above the cheap and shameless behavior of those who made him prisoner and put him to death.

Jesus reached Bethany on Friday afternoon. The Jewish sabbath began at six o'clock Friday afternoon and extended until the same hour Saturday. The Gospels do not mention any events on Saturday, but we may imagine Jesus going to the synagogue on the sabbath, as was his custom. We may assume also that he spent the remainder of the day resting in the home of Lazarus.

2. *Events on Sunday* (Mark 11:1–11; Matt. 21:1–17; Luke 19:29–44)

The first of Jesus' visits to the Holy City during the last week was made on Sunday. His entrance into the city on this occasion is usually called the triumphal entry. We often think of Jesus going to the city that day amid the peaceful quiet of our Sunday or sabbath. However, the Jewish sabbath was the day before, and the day of his entry would correspond to our Monday. The city was not quiet. It was densely crowded; the noisy multitude filled all available space. Jesus was the center of interest to the vast crowds surging on all sides. He was being acclaimed Messiah by these multitudes, though he knew that many who were then hailing him as Messiah would be shouting for his death a few days later.

Jesus went into the Temple and healed the blind and the lame who came to him. The children even took up the refrain and sang "Hosanna to the Son of David." Jesus allowed himself to be acclaimed as the Messiah. He had met the challenge of the Jews.

3. *Events on Monday* (Mark 11:12–19; Matt. 21:12–19; Luke 19:45–48; John 12:20–50)

After a night of rest in Bethany, Jesus and his disciples again set out for Jerusalem. Upon arriving in the city, Jesus went immediately to the Temple and cast out the merchants and money-changers. The most important event recorded on Monday was the significant visit of the Greeks for a conference with Jesus.

4. *Events on Tuesday* (Mark 11:19 to 12:44; Matt. 21:19 to 23:39; Luke 20)

Tuesday was one of the longest, hardest, and most decisive days in all the ministry of Jesus. Coming into the city early in the morning, he was occupied constantly until late at night, when he trudged wearily back to Bethany in the darkness. His enemies had prepared to challenge him, ensnare him, and discredit him by subtle questions. There were four different groups who, with carefully prepared questions, came to him in the Temple in the presence of the people. The questions appeared guileless, but their propounders had planned their attacks so, as they thought, Jesus could not possibly escape their snares.

Jesus was more than a match for these tricky men; he handled each situation so skillfully that his opponents were put to rout. Following these encounters, Jesus gave his terrible denunciation of the scribes and Pharisees and then delivered three long discourses. The Jews had now finally rejected him. He then left the city to return to Bethany.

The Gospels do not tell of any activities on Wednesday. We may imagine, however, that this was an important day both for Jesus and for his disciples. He would need quiet and rest after the strenuous days already spent and in view of what was to come. He would need time for prayer and meditation as he prepared "to go unto the Father." He would need also to devote himself to his disciples, who were always in his heart, in preparation for the events which they were unable to anticipate and understand.

5. *Events on Thursday and Thursday Night* (Mark 14:12–72; Matt. 26:17–75; Luke 22:7–65; John 13:1 to 18:57)

Thursday afternoon (according to the usually accepted chronology) Jesus joined his disciples in Jerusalem to eat the Passover meal at sunset. Here he gave his disciples an object lesson in humility, ate the Passover meal, and identified Judas as the betrayer. After this he instituted the Lord's Supper and then spent a long time in quiet talk with his disciples before going out to the Garden of Gethsemane just east of the Temple area. Here he experienced the terrible agony of tasting death for every man (see Heb. 2:9). At midnight the enemies of Jesus, led by Judas, came to arrest him. He was taken by them for a night of shameful treatment.

Between the time of his arrest and the hour of crucifixion (about 9:00 A.M. the next day) Jesus was led through a series of trials which were but legal "frame-ups."

There is always the danger that inexperienced students may assume that these trials were legitimate and that Jesus was guilty of some crime which merited punishment. But such was not the case. These trials were not legitimate, honest processes to establish the guilt or the innocence of the defendant. They were never intended to be fair, impartial efforts. They were legal conspiracies engineered by his enemies, not to secure a just verdict, but to secure the condemnation of Jesus. The Jews were determined to kill Jesus, and these trials were intended only to provide a legal justification. Every trial was filled with glaring illegalities.

During the early morning hours Peter made his denials, and Judas, realizing something of his sin, tried to return the money to the Jews. In despair he went out and hanged himself.

VIII. The Death of Jesus (Matt. 27; Mark 15; Luke 23; John 19)

With Jesus now in their possession his enemies heaped abuse upon him. He was mocked and scourged; they spat in his face and turned loose their sea of hatred upon him. He was forced to head the procession out to the place of crucifixion, bearing the cross on which he was to die. Beheading or stoning to death were the two usual forms of capital punishment employed by the Jews, but in this case they used the terrible form of crucifixion, which was regularly employed only in the case of the lowest class of criminals. The act of crucifixion affected none of the body's vital organs, so that death came slowly and with terrible physical anguish.

Jesus was placed on the cross about nine o'clock in the morning. During the three hours before noon a number of events transpired: Jesus uttered three sayings; the soldiers cast lots for his garments; the inscription was placed on the cross; the multitudes scoffed; the soldiers and others derided Jesus; and the penitent thief was saved.

Pilate, as an act of revenge on the Jews, had an inscription made to be placed on the perpendicular bar of the cross just above the head of Jesus. The words, "This is Jesus the king of the Jews" written in Hebrew, Greek, and Latin were thus displayed so that all could read them.

The Gospel writers have recorded seven sayings of Jesus on the cross. The first of these came in the early stages of crucifixion. The first three hours ended at noon. It was then that a thick darkness settled down over the earth, though the Syrian sun should have been at its brightest at this hour. As this strange darkness came, the multitudes were startled and fear possessed them. Many believed that this must be the power of God. The supernatural darkness lasted until three o'clock in the afternoon; then, as the hours dragged on, the darkness began to dissipate. In peaceful resignation Jesus calmly repeated the words of the psalmist, "Father, into thy hands I commend my spirit" (Luke 23:46). Having finished his work, "the unresting Saviour took his rest." Life left his body; his spirit returned to the Father.

The "Tragedy of the Ages" was finished. Within six hours after Jesus was placed on the cross he was dead, whereas victims usually lived for two or three days, dying by degrees. Since no vital organs were affected, crucifixion did not result in immediate death. We may reverently ask, What caused the death of Jesus? In one sense, the answer is that he died of a broken heart or a ruptured blood vessel. In an experience of intense emotional suffering the blood vessels may rupture and death ensues. The burden of the sin of the world—past, present, and future—broke the heart of Jesus. He bore the sin of the world, and it killed him. The final word is found in John 19:30 ASV. He "gave up [dismissed] his spirit." He willed to die (John 10:18).

The death of Jesus has tremendous significance for Christian people. Through the centuries since that time the great majority of his followers have placed his atoning death at the very center of Christian doctrine. This is the heart of the gospel. Only by his death could Jesus make atonement for sin and effect his work of redemption. Jesus was more than a noble martyr who was willing to die for a cause; he was the only begotten Son of God who died for the sins of the world.

He was pronounced dead before 6:00 P.M., and his body was taken down and placed in the tomb of Joseph, of Arimathea. A guard was stationed by the tomb, the door was sealed, and a large stone was rolled up against the door. This was about six o'clock in the afternoon; Jesus was dead and was in the tomb. His followers in desolation scattered through the city.

IX. VICTORY OVER DEATH (Matt. 28; Mark 16; Luke 24; John 20–21)

Jesus remained in the tomb Friday night, Saturday (the Jewish sabbath) and part of Sunday morning. According to Matthew, early Sunday morning there came a great earthquake; an angel of the Lord descended from heaven and opened the tomb. Jesus was raised from the dead by the power of God. Thus we have the most significant and important of all miracles.

Christ triumphed over death. The bewildered and griefstricken disciples got the assurance of this great reality as Jesus appeared to various groups on Sunday and in the following days. Altogether there are ten of these appearances of Jesus recorded in the New Testament. Paul says that Jesus "was seen of above five hundred brethren at once" (1 Cor. 15:6). The disciples, once so dejected and faithless, now became convinced beyond any question of the reality of Jesus' resurrection. They were transformed from a hesitant and timid group into a radiant and militant company who defied their enemies and proclaimed their faith with a courage unparalleled in all history. Christianity was on its way to conquer the world.

1. The Significance of the Resurrection

The resurrection of Jesus has far-reaching consequences. It is significant because of what it demonstrates. The resurrection proved Jesus' claim to deity and indicated his char-

acter. He was "declared to be the Son of God with power,
. . . by the resurrection from the dead" (Rom. 1:4 ASV).
His resurrection demonstrates the completion of redemption.
If he had remained in the tomb he could not have redeemed
the world. The fact that Jesus rose from the dead assures us
that he now lives and is in the hearts of believers. His resurrection is our assurance of life after death. This great miracle
guarantees final triumph for the believer, "Because I live,
ye shall live also" (John 14:19). "For if we have been
planted together in the likeness of his death, we shall be also
in the likeness of his resurrection" (Rom. 6:5).

2. Jesus, the Central Figure of the Human Race

While the earthly life of Jesus was a brief one of only
some thirty-three years, and his public ministry covered but
three years, no other man has ever influenced the world like
Jesus. This continuing influence is eloquently expressed in a
quotation which is often used, though the authorship of it
is not certainly known.

> Here is a man who was born in an obscure village, the child
> of a peasant woman. He grew up in another obscure village. He
> worked in a carpenter shop until He was thirty, and then for
> three years He was an itinerant preacher. He never wrote a
> book. He never held an office. He never owned a home. He
> never had a family. He never went to college. He never put His
> foot inside a big city. He never traveled two hundred miles
> from the place where He was born. He never did one of the
> things that usually accompany greatness. He had no credentials
> but Himself. . . . While still a young man, the tide of popular
> opinion turned against Him. His friends ran away. One of
> them denied Him. He was turned over to His enemies. He
> went through the mockery of a trial. He was nailed upon a cross
> between two thieves. His executioners gambled for the only
> piece of property He had on earth while He was dying—and
> that was His coat. When He was dead He was taken down and
> laid in a borrowed grave through the pity of a friend.
>
> Nineteen wide centuries have come and gone and today He
> is the centerpiece of the human race and the leader of . . .
> progress.
>
> I am far within the mark when I say that all the armies that

ever marched, and all the navies that were ever built, and all the parliaments that ever sat, and all the kings that ever reigned, put together, have not affected the life of man upon this earth as powerfully as has this One solitary life! [1]

SELECTED

FOR CLASS DISCUSSION AND FURTHER STUDY

1. Why is it important to believe in the incarnation and the virgin birth of Jesus?
2. Show how God's plan of redemption, which has been an unfolding story throughout the Old Testament, reached its fruition in Christ's atoning death.
3. Why do we believe in the bodily resurrection of Jesus? What bearing does this truth have on our expectations about our own resurrection bodies?

---

[1] "Greater Than Kings and Parliaments," *1000 Beautiful Things* (Chicago: Spencer Press, Inc., 1947), p. 424. Used by permission of publisher.

CHAPTER 9

9

The Design for World Conquest

JESUS CHRIST CAME into the world to establish a kingdom. Throughout his ministry the idea of the continuing expansion of the movement he was inaugurating is emphasized. He prepared and commissioned his disciples to assume leadership of this enterprise after his death. It was a movement with a program for the conquest of the world.

After the death, resurrection, and ascension of Jesus this enterprise was immediately begun. His followers tarried in Jerusalem until the Holy Spirit came on the day of Pentecost—ten days after his ascension—to empower them for this task. They had the assurance of his guidance and his presence. "And lo, I am with you always" (Matt. 28:20 ASV).

The book of Acts, written by Luke as a continuation of his Gospel, is our one authentic record of the marvelous achievements of these first disciples. The book makes no claim of giving a complete, detailed record of all that occurred, for this was impossible. It does give the main outlines of the progress made, with representative experiences.

Acts, after the brief introduction (1:1-3), falls naturally into three well-defined sections: First is the story of the development in Jerusalem itself (1:4 to 8:1). The next section (8:2 to 12:25) tells the story of the spread of the faith in the land of Palestine. The third section (13:1 to 28:31) is devoted mainly to the work of the apostle Paul among the Gentiles in the far places of the Roman Empire.

Following the four Gospels, which give the accounts of the earthly life of Jesus, all the rest of the New Testament deals with the expansion of the Christian movement. We shall trace this expansion up to approximately A.D. 100, when the New Testament account closes.

I. EXPANSION IN JERUSALEM (Acts 1:4 to 8:1)

After his resurrection Jesus appeared to various groups of believers over a period of forty days, after which he went back to the Father. The followers of Jesus tarried in prayer in Jerusalem for ten days, when on the day of Pentecost the Holy Spirit came. During this time Matthias was elected to take the place of Judas Iscariot.

On the great day of Pentecost, Peter, the accepted leader, interpreted the miracle of the coming of the Holy Spirit, then preached his famous sermon, during which about three thousand people were converted. With this remarkable event, the Christian movement was under way; a new day was at hand.

It is quite evident that a new force was at work in Jerusalem. The disciples had become a dynamic, courageous, and aggressive company, using every occasion for the propagation of their faith. Great numbers of people believed and were baptized. Miracles occurred with frequency, and the whole city was stirred.

A great church was organized in Jerusalem. Members were carefully instructed in the doctrines of Christ; they maintained fellowship with each other; they were unwavering in their attendance at prayers. They added others to their number through their personal witnessing.

Almost immediately these Christians were forced to endure severe persecution. The Jewish leaders tried in vain to stop the tide of Christian advance, but it continued as multitudes believed. The city of Jerusalem was stirred as one miracle after another marked the steady growth of the church. As the number of believers grew and added duties demanded the attention of the disciples, seven assistants (deacons) were elected "to serve tables" so that the disciples would be free to devote themselves wholly to spiritual matters. (Acts 6:1–8)

The bitter persecutions reached a climax in the martyrdom of Stephen (Acts 6:9 to 7:60). This event led to the dispersion of the Christians to various parts of the Roman Empire. In their effort to "break up" this new movement, the enemies of Christianity had "spread the fire."

II. Christianity Reaches Out into Palestine (Acts 8:4 to 12:25)

It was but natural that this marvelous new movement should flow out from Jerusalem into the regions round about. The book of Acts does not contain a full account of this expansion in Palestine. However, there are several events which are typical, no doubt, of what happened in the homeland of the Jews.

1. *The Ministry of Philip* (Acts 8:5–40)

To Philip, one of the seven deacons, belongs the honor of being the first missionary out of Jerusalem. As a result of the terrible persecutions, he "went down to the city of Samaria, and preached Christ." Philip was heartily received, and many responded to his message and were baptized. He was able also to perform many miracles. "And there was great joy in that city."

The church in Jerusalem heard of the successful mission of Philip in Samaria and sent Peter and John to confirm his work. They came and approved the work which was being done among these people. Upon the completion of their mission in the city of Samaria, Peter and John returned to Jerusalem, "and preached the gospel in many villages of the Samaritans."

Philip later went southward on the desert road that led to Gaza, where he met the Ethiopian eunuch. When the eunuch had been converted and baptized and had resumed his journey, Philip was caught away, "and passing through he preached in all the cities, till he came to Caesarea."

2. *Peter's Work on the Coast* (Acts 9:32 to 11:18)

Peter went to the region of Sharon on the Mediterranean coast, where he had notable success in Lydda and Joppa. Luke tells us that his work was "known throughout all Joppa: and many believed on the Lord" (ASV). One of the most significant of all Peter's experiences was in preaching in the home of Cornelius, the Roman centurion at Caesarea, when he and many other Gentiles were won to Christ. This event, with its subsequent influence on the thinking of leaders in the Jerusalem church (Acts 15:6–11) may be considered a pivotal point in the New Testament story of the expansion of Christianity to include the Gentiles.

3. *The Church in Antioch of Syria* (Acts 11:19–30)

Luke tells of the spread of the gospel among the Gentiles in another community which was soon to become a center from which the whole foreign mission enterprise was to be launched. It was in Antioch of Syria.

When the furious persecution after the death of Stephen occurred, some believers went up to Antioch to live. At first they spoke of Christ only to Jews, but later arrivals boldly proclaimed their faith to Greeks living in Antioch. Again the results were amazing, because a great number believed and were baptized. From this beginning a mighty Christian church, predominantly Greek, developed. They were active and aroused such opposition among the native people that they earned the nickname Christian, a derisive epithet which has come to be a designation honored and respected by the whole world.

III. CHRISTIANITY ENTERS THE GENTILE WORLD (Acts 13:1 to 28:31)

Luke devotes more than half of the book of Acts to the experiences of Paul and other apostles in taking the gospel "far hence unto the Gentiles" (Acts 22:21). This is the beginning of what we call "foreign missions." The commanding figure in this great enterprise was Paul. Because we shall now consider the work of the apostle who has been acclaimed as the greatest servant of the Son of man, it will be well to get something of the background and of the early life of this apostle.

Paul was born of Jewish parents in Tarsus of Cilicia, probably in the year A.D. 1. He was educated in Tarsus, and

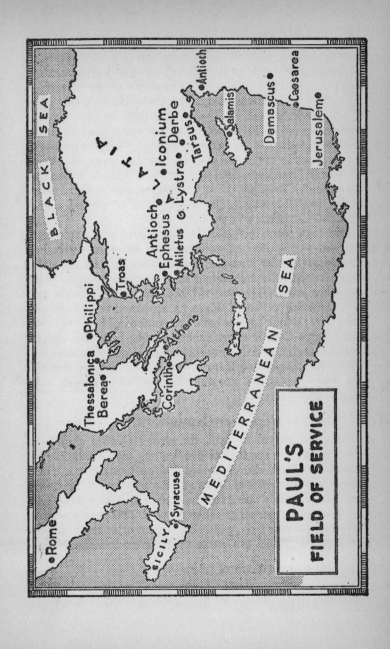

PAUL'S
FIELD OF SERVICE

in Jerusalem he took the customary training preparatory to becoming a rabbi. After completing his studies in Jerusalem, he went back to Tarsus, where he probably served as a rabbi.

When the Christian movement expanded so rapidly after the day of Pentecost, Paul was called back to Jerusalem to help stamp out this new sect, later known as Christians. He soon became the leader and employed the severest measures in the effort to crush the church. Having accomplished his purpose in Jerusalem, Saul was on the way up to Damascus to persecute Christians there, when he was miraculously converted, probably in A.D. 33. In Damascus he proved a very powerful Christian witness.

Paul then went to Arabia for meditation and study and, after two years, returned to Damascus, where he worked so effectively that the Jews forced him to flee the city. He went to Jerusalem, where he spent some two weeks with Peter and other leaders. He returned to Tarsus, not as a rabbi, but as a Christian preacher. Here he remained for some nine years, after which he was called to Antioch of Syria to serve in the large Gentile church there. It was from this church that the foreign mission enterprise moved out to reach Gentiles in Asia Minor and Europe. Indeed, we may say that the first foreign mission program by the early church was launched in Antioch.

IV. The First Missionary Campaign (Acts 13–15)

After the arrival of Saul, the strong Gentile church in Antioch had the services of five leading men (Acts 13:1). Naturally such a church would feel an interest in Gentile people in other regions. Through the ministry of Barnabas and Saul, the Holy Spirit led the church to realize its obligation to take the gospel to other peoples. This strong church served as a center from which three great campaigns for proclaiming the gospel to Gentile people were launched.

1. Going to the Gentiles (Acts 13)

As we begin our study of this first campaign, it will be helpful to get a glimpse of it as a whole. There were three men to go on this first journey: Barnabas, Saul, and a young man from Jerusalem named John Mark. The campaign lasted from the spring of the year A.D. 47 to the summer or fall of A.D. 49. The missionaries departed from Antioch of Syria and went down to the port of Seleucia, where they took ship and sailed to the island of Cyprus. Their first stop was at Salamis on the east coast of the island. They worked westward through the island to the city of Paphos.

From this port they sailed north to the mainland of Asia, landing at Perga in Pamphylia. Here John Mark deserted the company and returned to Jerusalem. Paul and Barnabas went up in the highlands to Antioch of Pisidia. After a period here they went eastward to Iconium, then south a few miles to Lystra, and thence later to Derbe, a short distance eastward. Retracing their steps, they returned to the cities where young churches had been started and were now functioning in the heart of Asia: Lystra, Iconium, and Antioch in Psidia. After confirming the brethren and leading the churches to complete their organization (Acts 14:22–23), they went on to Perga, and then to the port of Attalia, from whence they sailed to Seleucia. The trip from Seleucia up to Antioch of Syria completed their campaign. This was the shortest of the three missionary campaigns, but it was a notable start in the evangelizing of the Gentile world.

When at last the missionaries reached home and "gathered the church together, they rehearsed all that God had done with them, and how he had opened door of faith unto the Gentiles." What a wonderful story they had to tell of their two long years of labor among the Gentiles.

2. The Great Council at Jerusalem (Acts 15)

Shortly after their return to Antioch (Syria), the apostles learned of a very dangerous situation which had developed in their absence. Earlier, certain brethren from Jerusalem (without the authority of the Jerusalem church) had come up to Antioch and had insisted that a Gentile man could not become a Christian without first submitting to the ancient Jewish rite of circumcision. This teaching was both unjust and unjustified. Paul saw the danger and took charge of the situation. Since the brethren who raised the question were from Jerusalem, and since it was highly desirable for the leaders at Jerusalem to be rightly informed, the issue was taken to Jerusalem where, in a large council, the matter was debated and settled. Paul won his fight, insisting that no such rite was necessary. A man becomes a believer in Christ by personal faith and not by any man-made ceremony. In this matter the Holy Spirit worked through Paul to save Christianity from a policy that would have shackled it and handicapped the progress of the Christian movement.

V. THE SECOND MISSIONARY CAMPAIGN (Acts 15:36 to 18:22)

1. *Dispute over John Mark* (Acts 15:36–41)

Upon their return to Antioch from Jerusalem, Paul and Barnabas could not longer resist the urge to get back among the Gentiles. Unfortunately a misunderstanding arose which separated these two great leaders. John Mark, who had deserted on the first campaign, wanted to accompany them on this journey. Barnabas was agreeable, but Paul would not consent. The outcome was that Barnabas took John with him and returned to Cyprus. Paul took Silas as his companion for his second campaign.

2. *Experiences in Asia and Europe* (Acts 15:40 to 18:22)

This campaign was much longer and covered a greater distance than the first. The members of the party were Paul, Silas, Timothy, and Luke, although these were not all together at all times. The campaign started in the year 50 and lasted approximately three years. Paul and Silas started from Antioch, the home base, and went overland to Tarsus, from whence they traveled to Derbe, Lystra, Iconium, and Antioch (Pisidia), revisiting the cities included in the first journey.

From Troas on the coast, they went across the Aegean Sea to Philippi. The missionary movement had reached Greece, in Europe. From Philippi Paul went to Thessalonica,

Berea, Athens, and Corinth. In these European cities they labored long and successfully though they were severely persecuted. Strong churches were founded at Philippi, Thessalonica, Berea, and Corinth.

It was now A.D. 53 and Paul had been away from his home base three years. He was eager to get back to Syrian Antioch to learn of conditions there and to get news from other churches where he had worked. Apparently Paul left Silas and Timothy at Corinth. It may be, as some think, that they then returned to Macedonia. At any rate, Paul left Corinth accompanied only by Aquilla and Priscilla. Going through the port of Cenchreae they came to Ephesus, where Aquila and Priscilla remained. In Ephesus Paul went into the synagogue and reasoned with the Jews. After this brief stop he went on to Jerusalem. Leaving Jerusalem he went to Antioch, from whence he and Silas had gone three years earlier on this extended campaign among the Gentiles.

A new development took place during the second missionary campaign; Paul wrote the first two of his epistles: 1 and 2 Thessalonians. Later on he was to write nearly a dozen more letters, which became a vital part of our New Testament. Each of these letters was written to deal with a particular situation. They served effectively in doing this, and they also constitute the best authoritative statements of Christian doctrine. They are our greatest theological treasures.

VI. The Third Missionary Campaign (Acts 18:23 to 21:16)

Paul tarried in Antioch but briefly before setting forth on his third campaign. This campaign was, with the exception of his long sojourn in Ephesus and his visit to Illyricum, mainly spent in places where he had previously worked. He went overland from Antioch to Cilicia, Phrygia, and Galatia. He moved from here to Ephesus, the capital of Asia, for a long stay. Leaving Ephesus he went back through Macedonia, on to Illyricum and then to Corinth, where the campaign was considered finished. From here he returned to Macedonia, thence to Troas, to Miletus, and thence to Tyre, Caesarea, and finally to Jerusalem. The dates are A.D. 53 to 57 or 54 to 58. He had a large number of helpers during this period, no one of whom was with him all the time.

The third campaign was devoted not so much to direct evangelization, except at Ephesus, as to teaching the Gentile churches which had been established. It was during the years of this journey that the apostle developed and expounded what we call "Pauline theology." During this time he wrote Galatians, 1 and 2 Corinthians, and Romans. He came to grips with all the current false systems of religion and, in the heat of conflict, produced the greatest of all doctrinal treatises. Unquestionably Paul, through the tutorage of the Holy Spirit, became the greatest interpreter of the gospel of Jesus Christ. Indeed, he was the first real interpreter. It was his responsibility to systematize and expound Christianity as a way of life and as a system of theological thought.

VII. PAUL IN PRISON (Acts 21 : 17 to 28 : 31)

After four long years among the Gentile Christians, Paul was eager to get back to Jerusalem and Antioch. As he journeyed homeward, he was repeatedly warned of impending disaster awaiting him in Jerusalem. Despite all these warnings he was determined to go.

1. *Arrested and Held* (Acts 21 : 17 to 26 : 32)

After arriving in Jerusalem, Paul and his friends reported to James and the leaders of the church on his work among the Gentile churches, and delivered to them the money he had collected on this journey for the needy Christians in Jerusalem. James or some of the other leaders then told Paul of the plot of certain Jews in Jerusalem to kill him. Despite all precautions taken by Paul, he was arrested and was forced to undergo the most trying experiences. Of course Paul was innocent of the charges made against him but the outcome was five long years in prison.

In order to protect Paul from the mob, the authorities

transferred him to Caesarea, where he was tried by both Felix and Festus. He was not released, as he should have been, and remained here two years. He appealed his case to Caesar and was taken by ship to Rome.

2. Paul in Rome (Acts 27-28)

The account of the long journey, with the shipwreck and a winter's stay on the island of Melita (Malta), is given in detail in Acts 27-28.

Paul had long dreamed of visiting Rome, but had hoped to come as a free man. He now entered Rome as a prisoner chained to a guard. He was given the privilege of living in "his own hired house" as he awaited trial. He used his time in a remarkably effective ministry over all the city, counseling with Christians and winning new converts. During his stay in Rome he wrote four epistles: Philippians, Ephesians, Colossians, and Philemon.

We have no record of Paul's trial. In fact Luke closes the book of Acts abruptly with the statement, "And he abode two whole years in his own hired dwelling [at his own expense], and received all that went in unto him, preaching the kingdom of God, and teaching the things concerning the Lord Jesus Christ with all boldness, none forbidding him" (Acts 28:30-31 ASV).

We have no historical record of what came later. The majority of scholars hold that Paul was released and then spent the next four or five years visiting his churches and working throughout the Roman Empire. It is believed that in the fierce persecutions under Emperor Nero, Paul was arrested as a leader of the Christians, was tried in Rome on the charge of disloyalty to the Roman Government, and was beheaded, probably in the year A.D. 67. In view of all the circumstances it seems that this is probably what occurred.

It was during the interval between Paul's imprisonments that he wrote 1 Timothy and Titus. While he was in a Roman prison awaiting death, he wrote 2 Timothy, the last of his letters.

At the time of his death Paul could count many strong

churches in the Roman Empire, where many thousands of loyal Christians were enlisted in the enterprise of making the world Christian. Paul is generally regarded as the greatest man in Christian history, next to the Son of man.

VIII. COMPLETING THE STORY

Luke, the author of Acts, traced the general development of the Christian movement in Jerusalem and Palestine (Acts 1–12). When he came to the work of Paul among the Gentiles he let the other Christian leaders like Peter, James, John, Barnabas, John Mark, and others drop out of his narrative. We do not have a complete historical record of the later work of these men. However we do know a little about the activities of Peter, James, and John in these later years of New Testament history.

1. *Later Work of James, Peter, and John*

James continued as the leader of the church in Jerusalem and was known as "the righteous." Tradition says that he was so constant in prayer that his knees became like those of a camel.

Peter, despite his weaknesses, was one of the most influential New Testament leaders. He seems to have served as a missionary to the Jews of the dispersion and to have been in Asia at one time (1 Cor. 5:9). The question of his being in Rome is still highly controversial. Tradition says that he was crucified head downward at his own request.

John spent many years in Asia where he was known as the gentle "apostle of love." He was regarded as the most influential Christian in this area. He was exiled on Patmos, where he wrote the Apocalypse. One of the traditions is that he too, when nearly one hundred years old, died as a martyr by being submerged in a caldron of boiling oil.

2. *The General Epistles and the Apocalypse*

There are eight so-called general epistles in the New Testament which deserve a word of comment: James; 1 and 2 Peter; 1, 2, and 3 John; Jude; and Hebrews. Each of these letters was written for a specific purpose. James is perhaps the earliest of all these and was written by James the leader of the church in Jerusalem. Peter wrote his two epistles to Jewish Christians, probably in Asia. John's three letters, while very brief, were intended to encourage the Christians in Asia. We do not know who wrote Hebrews, the great argument for the superiority of Christianity over Judaism. The little book of Jude was written by Jude, the half brother of Jesus.

The Apocalypse, or the book of Revelation, closes the New Testament. It is generally held that John, the great apostle of love, wrote the book of Revelation while in exile on the isle of Patmos.

3. Conclusion

The New Testament closes about A.D. 100. The records indicate that Christian churches were established in every part of the Mediterranean world. Despite the hardships endured by Christians, they continued to multiply. We may not know the number in these churches though we may be sure that there were many thousands of them.

Thus when the New Testament closes we find Christian churches established in practically all parts of the Roman Empire. This movement began very modestly but the growth it attained in less than one hundred years gave promise of greater conquests to come later. To use the language of Jesus, the mustard seed was already growing to become a tree. We recognize the fact that the progress made by Christianity during these 1900 years has not been as great as we could wish, but it does encourage us in the hope for ultimate conquest. We may, therefore, cherish the expectation that it will yet be true that "the kingdoms of this world are become the kingdoms of our Lord, and of his Christ; and he shall reign for ever and ever" (Rev. 11:15).

We have now completed our survey of Bible history. We have been able to get only a "bird's-eye view" of the big events in this history. It is our hope that this survey may inspire every reader to make a more detailed and intensive study of this remarkable book which we rightly call the Word of God and the Book of books.

FOR CLASS DISCUSSION AND FURTHER STUDY

1. Show how Acts 1:8 may be considered an outline of the spread of the message of redemption, which you have traced through the whole Bible. The New Testament uses the imagery of a relay race when it says of the saints of old, "They without us should not be made perfect" (Heb. 11:40). The message has been handed to us by the "runners" who have preceded us. Will we run and pass it on or let it drop from our hands?

2 On an appropriate map trace each of Paul's missionary journeys, counting the times he revisited churches. Why did he place so much emphasis on return visits?

Questions for Review and Examination

CHAPTER 1

1. Why does the Bible continue to be the world's most popular book?
2. What is meant by the inspiration of the Scriptures?

CHAPTER 2

3. Why are the first three chapters of Genesis so significant?
4. Indicate evidences of Abraham's faith which help to explain why he is held up as an example of one who believed God (Rom. 4:1-16).
5. Point out some of the elements of weakness and strength in the career of Jacob.
6. Show how Joseph was used of God to preserve his people.

CHAPTER 3

7. Show how God prepared Moses for his work.
8. Why is the law of Moses so important?
9. List some of the miracles in the experiences of Moses.
10. Discuss Joshua's plan for conquering Canaan.
11. Why is the period of the judges known as the dark ages?

CHAPTER 4

12. Show how Samuel served the people of Israel
13. Show the results of sin in Saul's life.
14. Point out the good qualities of David as king.
15. Tell how Solomon made a good beginning as king of Israel.

CHAPTER 5

16. What was the fatal sin of the rulers of the Northern Kingdom?
17. Discuss the fall of Samaria and the captivity of the Northern Kingdom.
18. Give the cause of the decline and fall of Judah.

CHAPTER 6

19. Discuss the life of the Hebrew people in Babylonian exile.
20. What made it possible for these exiles to return to Jerusalem? Name the three leaders who took groups back to the homeland.

21. Name three prophets who helped the people during the exile.
22. Indicate the importance of the period "between the Testaments."

Chapter 7

23. Name the books of poetry in the Old Testament. What is the chief purpose of the Psalms?
24. Give the setting for the work of Amos and Hosea.
25. Discuss the message of Isaiah.
26. Tell of the ministry of Jeremiah.

Chapter 8

27. What is meant by the incarnation and the virgin birth of Jesus?
28. Why did the Jews oppose Jesus?
29. What is meant by the atoning death of Jesus?
30. Tell of some of the appearances of Jesus after his resurrection.

Chapter 9

31. What is the purpose and value of the book of Acts?
32. Show the significance of Paul's epistles. Name the authors, other than Paul, who wrote New Testament epistles.
33. Tell of the last days and death of Paul.
34. Name New Testament leaders, other than Paul and his companions, who made significant contributions to the spread of Christianity.